BLAKES: CREATED BY ANOUSKA HEMPEL

With special thanks to our photographers

Ditmar Bollaert
Mieke Coghe
Annelies de Mey
Phile Deprez
Vincent Gyselinck
Karel Moortgat
Lieven Nollet
Jan Van Goidsenhoven

&

Hub. Kenens
Concept and lay-out

Compiled, written and edited by Luc Quisenaerts
Concept and lay-out Hub. Kenens
Printed by Nauwelaerts
Pre-press Beeldspraak
Photographs see p. 190
Assistance with Dutch editing Theo Jochems
English translation Owen Davis
French editing Philippe & Jérôme Bockiau

ISBN 90-76124-01-9   D/1997/8101/2

First Edition

HOTEL GEMS
IN
GREAT BRITAIN AND IRELAND

COMPILED, WRITTEN AND EDITED BY

LUC QUISENAERTS

PUBLISHERS D-PUBLICATIONS

THE SERIES
'HOTEL GEMS IN THE WORLD'

Dear reader,

After 'Hotel Gems in France', this 'Hotel Gems in Great Britain and Ireland' is the second book in a unique series.

Each book will describe the rich and fascinating hotel heritage of a certain country, a group of countries or a continent.

Each country will be described from a very special, original angle.

By enjoying the hospitality of the people of a country for one or several nights, one can taste the history, the culture and the cuisine of such a country in a deeply personal way. Therefore, we thank all the hotels who co-operated in this project for offering their hospitality, which is usually reserved for the guests who stay there, to the readers of these books.

In the following months and years, we hope to offer you a whole series of new voyages of discovery to the most fascinating hotels in the world.

We intend to enable the readers to 'walk' through all these gems, to discover their unique nooks and crannies, by leafing through each book.

That is why this series, and each book in itself, can be considered a valuable archive containing a piece of the wealth and beauty of a country, created by the passion of all those people who put their souls into it.

...

HOTEL GEMS
IN
GREAT BRITAIN AND IRELAND

This is going to be a journey through time, through history. On our travels, we will meet many illustrious figures: mythical ones, such as King Arthur and Merlin the Magician, and historic ones such as William the Conqueror, Henry VIII, the Duke of Buckingham, Queen Elizabeth I, the infamous Cromwell, Shakespeare, the Scottish freedom fighter Rob Roy, Queen Victoria and the Prince of Wales.
But we will also be fascinated by artists such as John Constable and landscape artists such as Capability Brown and Gertrude Jekyll.

Present-day personalities will tell their story and lead us through their hotels, such as the Duchess of Devonshire, Gerald Grosvenor, the Duke of Westminster, the famous designer Anouska Hempel, Roger Saul, founder of the Mulberry empire, Sir Bernard Ashley and many others.

Great Britain has always been an island with a very personal character, but at the same time it was the centre of a large empire, in which many foreign influences could be felt. Yet, it has preserved its own traditions as no other nation has. Four countries in one: England, Scotland, Wales and Northern Ireland, each with its own culture and customs, with London, the gigantic, bustling metropolis on the Thames, as its crown jewel. In great contrast to all this is Ireland: independent, but through its history so closely related to its big cousin. The emerald isle is so much smaller, but melancholy, unspoilt and touchingly beautiful.

This great wealth is reflected in the hotel world. We stay in thousand-year-old castles which have withstood time, on vast estates where romantic and dramatic events have taken place, in historic inns where the fate of a country was decided. We sample the wonderful cuisine in select Gentlemen's Clubs and find a touch of British colonial exoticism in the most trendy designer hotels where the 'beautiful people' stay. We sip tea by the fire in libraries or intimate lounges in hunting lodges, and play snooker in stately country houses. We walk in immense green parks and look out on gorgeous, rolling golf courses, play croquet on green lawns, go hunting in the vast woods of manor houses and fish for trout and salmon in mountain streams. We sleep in idyllic cottages with walled kitchen gardens and a murmuring river, we dine beside a waterfall and step into a 'real' fairy-tale.

Behind every façade, every garden hedge, lies a wonderful world, a world that we will explore in words and pictures.

Luc Quisenaerts
The author

THE COLLECTION

01

STON EASTON PARK

They had come from London, Paris and Brussels, the well-heeled gentlemen of the press with their canes and bowler hats. For a very special event was taking place in Ston Easton Park near Bath - the first automobile race ever was starting here on this sunny day in June 1906.

For long minutes, photographers stood on the lush green lawn, their heads under the black cloth of their cameras, and tried to immortalise the row of cars which were parked in front of a wonderful Palladian manor house.

There must have been a residence here in the Middle Ages, but the house as we know it now was built in 1740 by John Hippisley-Coxe and his wife Mary Northleigh of Peamore in Devon. Their son, Richard, was a highly cultivated person and, apart from being 'Knight of the Shire for the county

of Somerset' he involved himself in the refurbishment of the house. Richard, however, died young and his brother Henry inherited a wonderful estate – and many debts.

In spite of this, Henry managed to raise funds to commission Humphrey Repton, the famous landscape architect to design the park. In his famous 'Red Book', Repton wrote and sketched instructions on how to landscape the garden.

After Henry's death in 1795, his widow, Elizabeth, married Sir John Cox-Hippisley, a diplomat and politician. As a representative of King George II in Rome, Sir John devoted all his energy to the promulgation of Catholicism. For example, it was he who arranged for the Stuart jewels to be returned to

England and it was he who persuaded Parliament to grant Prince Henry, Cardinal of York, a generous pension when Napoleon's troops, after their occupation of Rome, had stopped the prelate from receiving any further funds. Elizabeth herself was an extraordinary woman, who had seen the consequences of her former brother-in-law Richard's mismanagement, and ruled over Ston Easton Park with iron discipline. Lady Hippisley also installed a laboratory where she conducted experiments with medicines. Sir John went as far as having a wall built to keep the obnoxious odours from invading the rest of the house.

Lady Hippisley also had a unique bathroom built in the octagonal room, adorned with statues, underneath a domed ceiling with a blue sky and golden stars. The room is still there, but the plunge bath itself has been boarded over.

After that, Ston Easton Park was handed down from one branch of the family to another. At the dawn of this centu-

One owner followed another and each contributed something to its restoration. Among them was Lord Rees-Mogg, former Editor of The Times.

In the end it was Mr and Mrs Peter Smedley who completed the restoration work. Having used Ston Easton Park as their private residence for a while, the Smedleys decided to

ry the resident Hippisleys, with Commander Richard John Bayntun Hippisley as head of the family, were passionately interested in inventions and mechanics. And that brings us back to the beginning of our story.

During World War II Queen Mary, who was visiting the area, expressed an explicit wish to go to Ston Easton and despite the fact that her household remarked that the castle looked rather neglected, she went to have tea there. During her visit, she admired a honey spoon which the Commander had fashioned from an old coin, and she was given the spoon to take home to Buckingham Palace as a souvenir.

After the Commander's death, Ston Easton Park became more and more delapidated and the contents were sold at public auction. Subsequently the house was vandalised, the lead stripped from the roof and many of the fireplaces,brassware and fittings stolen. Luckily in 1958, just in time, the house became the subject of a Preservation Order.

turn it into a spectacular hotel.

Their efforts were rewarded: in their opening year, they were given the 'Egon Ronay Hotel of the Year Award'.

This is not really surprising, for so many things are unique here - the magnificent collection of furniture and paintings, the delightful atmosphere generated within the house, in complete contrast to the distinctively austere façade, the refinement of the interior architecture and the exquisite cuisine, to name but a few.

The surroundings are just as unique.

Near the castle is a rippling river, with an arched stone bridge, which flows past the 17th century 'Gardener's Cottage'. It is an extremely idyllic little house in a very special spot, next to the romantic vegetable garden, and it contains two luxurious suites.

At night, the rustle of curious foxes and the calling of the owls will only be drowned by the whispering sound of the river flowing by.

14

The refined interior is in striking contrast to the austere façade. On the right, 'The Saloon'.

02

THE SLOANE HOTEL

On that rainy November evening, a thick fog came downstream from the Thames valley, spreading itself like a blanket over 19th century London. From the forest of chimneys in Chelsea, the smoke of coal-fires rose straight into the sky. The clatter of horses' hooves and the rattle of wooden coach wheels on the wet cobblestones could be heard.

The coachmen in their black suits and bowler hats drove their last rich guests safely home after an evening at the opera or the theatre. Apart from the steam whistle of the last train leaving nearby Victoria Station, nothing else could be heard.

Draycott Place, a street of beautiful red brick Victorian houses, was deserted. The night watchmen began to extinguish the street-lamps and most of the houses were dark.

But at number 29, the gas lights were still burning and if you were to glance inside you would have seen the people who lived there. A couple were sitting by the fire in the drawing room, and the maid in her white lacy apron was serving tea to the lady and brandy to the gentleman.

The lady was happily doing embriodery and the gentleman was reading the paper, a pipe in his mouth. The room was very cosy, with rich curtains, beautiful furniture, precious china and silver. The walls were hung with etchings, drawings and paintings depicting great moments and important people in the history of England: Elizabeth I, Lord Nelson, Wellington and the Battle of Waterloo, even a portrait of Queen Victoria, queen at the time, under whose reign Great Britain had grown into 'The Empire', the greatest power of all time.

The gentleman of the house, by the way, was interested in whatever might be happening in the furthest reaches where Great Britain ruled, and read the papers every day.

To him, India, Australia, South Africa and even the Virgin Islands seemed less remote than the grinding poverty of the suburbs of his own city.

What he could never have suspected is that some hundred years later, his house, more than any other house in Chelsea, would exude the atmosphere of the times in which he lived.

That is thanks to Sue Rogers, a famous interior designer who turned the house into an exquisite little hotel, with a dozen rooms and suites.

With the same care she would have used for her own home, Mrs. Rogers chose every item of the decoration at antique auctions and design markets. Each room is a masterpiece, furnished with beautiful fabrics and lace bedspreads.

But whether you stay in the Tricia Guild Suite with its four-poster bed, or in the neo-classic room where everything is decorated in the colour of caramelised sugar, each room exudes the atmosphere of the Victorian era.

The hotel has one highly original feature, which is unique in Great Britain and maybe the whole world.

Sue Rogers tells us: "It may seem incredible, but in The Sloane Hotel, you can sleep in one of our wonderful four-poster beds, and if you like it, you can buy it and have it delivered to your home."

This hotel is really one huge antiques and interior decoration shop, for nearly everything is for sale. We got the idea when we saw that the guests were full of admiration for the decor. And one of them begged us to be allowed to buy an etching that hung over his bed. One thing followed another: an antique caraffe, silver, china, paintings, old trunks, bedspreads, mahogany wardrobes."

Most items are unique, which is in particular interest to certain guests.

In the intimate reception room there is even a glass cabinet where cigarette holders, crocodile skin handbags and many Louis Vuitton products are discreetly displayed.

And Sue finds it fascinating to keep looking for new objects that suit the atmosphere of the hotel.

However not everything is for sale: the rare nineteenth-century admiral dress uniform for instance, and the precious reception desk which was made specially for the hotel by Viscount Linley.

These are simply too dear to the interior decorator-cum-hotelier, and they have become part of the image of The Sloane.

You can sleep and dine in your room at The Sloane Hotel,

but also browse as if you were in an antique shop…

19

03

ASHDOWN PARK HOTEL

Deep in the woods of Ashdown Forest, in the county of East Sussex, the forest suddenly changes into beautifully landscaped parkland, and an impressive lane leads to a monumental, stylish Victorian building from the 1860s.

It is surrounded by ponds, lawns, rivers and secret gardens. Nobody knows the exact date of the first building in the park, which at the time extended to no less than 3,563 acres and which comprised, among other things, an army range. Was it built under Thomas Bradford, who took possession of the estate in 1815, or was it built by Admiral Jacob Henniker, who was the owner of Ashdown Park from 1822 onwards?

Whatever the case may be, the fact is that Mr Thomas Charles Thompson, Member of Parliament for Durham, bought the estate in 1867. He had the existing manor house pulled down and started from scratch with the creation of what would one day become one of the most monumental hotels in England.

A park was landscaped, with wonderful big trees which still cast their shadows over the green of the golf course that stretches all the way up to the hotel. In 1886 he even had a small church built, so that his family and servants did not have to travel to Hartfield to perform their Sunday duties. And generous as he was, he housed the local village school in his castle, and provided free food for the children.

Thomas Charles Thompson died in 1892. In his will, he decreed that each of the servants of the castle should be given a black outfit, so that they could attend the funeral suitably dressed.

When World War I broke out, his grandson Captain Fisher vacated the castle and left it in the hands of Lady Brassey, who converted it to a hospital, where wounded Belgian officers could rest and recover.

Captain Fisher died in 1917 and the castle was put up for sale by his heirs.

After the war, a certain Sister Mary of the Order of Notre Dame from Namur in Belgium appeared as an angel of rescue. She came from the rich English Towneley dynasty and entered the convent in Belgium. Her Mother Superior sent her to the country of her birth in order to find a place of retreat for the Novices of the Order.

With the money from Sister Mary, who had, in the meantime, inherited the family fortune, and with the work and efforts of the Sisters, Ashdown Park became one of the most breathtakingly beautiful estates in England.

Several side wings were added and a magnificent church was erected: the Church of Our Lady and St.Richard, to the honour of Richard Towneley, the benefactor.

21

Marble was brought in from Italy, Switzerland and Sweden, the sculpted 'Way of the Cross' came from Bruges. The multi-coloured windows, with no less than 35 shades of blue, were a creation of the famous Harry Clarke of Dublin, and the stained glass was commissioned from Geoffrey Webb.

For a full fifty years Ashdown Park was a place of peace, contemplation and beauty. Then, first the Unites States International University and after that Barclays Bank took over the estate, the first for scientific cultural research, the second for an up-market training centre for the bank's executives. In 1993 the estate was sold to the present owners, who con-

verted it into a luxury hotel. Ashdown Park is a wonderful blend of the influences of all the previous residents and owners. It is as if the spirits of benefactors like Thomas Charles Thompson and Sister Mary still dwell there.

There is a feeling of the serenity of the Sisters of the Order of Notre Dame, but also an atmosphere of the world of international bankers and university lecturers who exchanged thoughts in a sympathetic environment, far from the hustle and bustle of daily life.

There is one thing that all the residents had in common: Ashdown Park was a place where they felt at home.

And the present hosts do everything within their power to convey this special atmosphere to everyone who visits the hotel. Not only is there the splendid golf course; there is also the Country Club, with an indoor pool, sauna and beauty parlour. Moreover, Ashdown is an ideal starting point for excursions into the surroundings - to the coastal town of Brighton with its wonderful pavilion, for instance, to the famous Glyndebourne Opera House, to Tunbridge Wells with its unique arcades and to the castles and gardens of Knole, Sissinghurst, Hever Castle and Chartwell, Winston Churchill's residence...to name just a few.

Space and endless peace in the religious, intellectual atmosphere of bygone days.

04

MICHAELS NOOK

When you arrive at Michaels Nook, you knock on the door or ring the bell and wait a while, as if you are visiting someone you know. After a few moments, Reg Gifford or a member of the staff comes to the door to welcome you. And when you look around, you wonder whether this is really an hotel...

There is no reception area, no ringing phones. Nothing but a splendid room with oriental carpets on the polished parquet floor, precious antiques everywhere, a grandfather clock and fresh flowers wherever you look. The notion of an 'hotel' in the

strict sense of the word does not apply here. For this is a gem of homely cosiness, which you enjoy from the moment you arrive until you are waved goodbye, leaving with the firm promise that you will certainly return.

Here, you are part of an English family, and are submerged in the unforgettable country atmosphere of the turn of the century. You have tea by the open fire in the lounge, where antique pianos in polished wood stand patiently waiting for a guest with musical talent. Great Danes lie down next to you and exotic cats purr by the crackling fire.

Here, comfortably ensconced in the cosy settee, your can reflect on the history of Michaels Nook and the life of the person who created all this beauty. The early Victorian manor house near Grasmere was built in 1859, in countryside of unforgettable beauty,.

Close by is Dove Cottage, where writer and poet William Wordsworth spent some of his most inspired years, and which is now a fascinating museum. The name 'Michaels Nook', by the way, derives from one of his poems: the one about Michael, the poor shepherd, who lived here all his life.

Apart from the heritage of the famous lyric poet,

it is also Reg Gifford's hotel which makes many people want to visit this small town in the Lake District.

Mr. Gifford's love of the area around Grasmere stems from the time when he visited it as a young man and keen cyclist from Blackpool. Later, when he had become a successful antiques dealer and restaurateur in Grasmere.

He opened his home 'Michaels Nook' as a country house hotel..

He kept the exterior in the style typical of the area, and with his experience as an antiques dealer, he recreated the Victorian era inside.

Ornamental plaster on the walls and ceilings, cladding of superior wood, china, crystal chandeliers - everything recalls the life of rich citizens of the time. A mahogany staircase with finely-carved banisters leads to twelve rooms and two suites. Several rooms have been embellished with lovely satinwood, others with mahogany, oak and even Chinese lacquer.

The luxurious bathrooms contain fluffy bathrobes and toiletries by Floris.

In the restaurant, the chef serves food of the same refinement as the rest of the hotel: fresh produce of superior quality are combined in gastronomic dishes which are artistically presented.

We sit by the fire, and enjoy the atmosphere, and order another English cup of tea and cakes, and do some armchair travelling through the locality. Michaels Nook stands right in the middle of the Lake District, an area of outstanding beauty, which lies within the counties of Cumbria and Lancashire.

The area, with its dozens of lakes, often dotted with small islands, such as Derwentwater, and lovely towns and villages such as Windermere and Hawkshead, is a perfect holiday destination.

We breathe in the fresh country air and enjoy the fairytale beauty of the thirteen-acre estate, surrounded by rugged green mountains.

From here, you can enjoy wonderful walks - to Dove Cottage, for instance, where in 1800 a poem was written with a goosefeather pen, beginning: "Upon a forest side at Grasmere Vale there dwelt a shepherd, Michael was his name."

05

AMBERLEY CASTLE

Our story begins in the year 682 A.D., when the Saxon king Caedwalla donated the 'Land of Amberley' to Wilfred, first bishop of Selsey. It was this Wilfred who brought Christianization to this part of the world. It was he himself, by the way, who converted the king to Christianity.

Later, the area became the property of the archbishop of Chichester and in the 12th century Bishop Luffa built a manor house there, the oldest part of the imposing castle.

In the year 1377 King Richard II granted Bishop William Rede the right to build the majestic ramparts and defence towers as a protection against, among others, the French pirates who sailed up the river Avon to Amberley.

This bishop has made a lasting impression on the history of Amberley Castle, if only by building the Great Hall, the best preserved 'dungeon' in England, the kitchen on the north wall, outside the ramparts (as a fire precaution), and a bathroom which was revolutionary for its time and which is still as good as intact, but which fortunately no longer needs to be used by present hotel guests.

Between 1508 and 1536, Bishop Sherborne, the last in a long line of bishops, lived in the castle. It was he who had two floors converted; one into the magnificent Queen's Room with its barrel vaulted ceiling, the other into the Great Room with its oak floor and ornaments.

One century later, the castle was dragged into the violence of the Civil war when Cromwell sent troops to Amberley in order to try and obtain taxes that had been held back by the royalist John Goring, resident of Amberley at the time.

Thus, the Great Hall was reduced to a ruin and some of the 14th century buildings were destroyed.

Amberley Castle received several royal visitors. John Goring, for instance, invited Charles II, who stayed there on October 14th, 1651 on his journey to France after the battle of Worcester.

Later, in 1683, he stayed there again, and on that occasion Sir James Brisco, who was Lord of the castle at the time, had a mural painted in the Queen's Room which depicted Charles II and Queen Catharina of Braganza at a hunting party.

This fresco is flanked by the king's and queen's coats of arms and has recently been beautifully restored.

During the following centuries, residents and conquerors came and went, including Queen Elisabeth 1 who owned the castle between 1588 and 1603. In 1893, the fifteenth Duke of Norfolk bought Amberley and started restoration works to the impressive gatehouse and west wall. He also decorated the King Charles Room with fancy wood panelling which exists to this day.

But the gates of the castle remained closed to the outside world and the noble residents lived their lives of quiet leisure, undisturbed.

That changed in 1988, when Joy and Martin Cummings bought the castle and made their dream of a lifetime come true - to transform an historic castle into a splendid Country House Hotel.

They have captured the atmosphere of the castle and its inhabitants through the ages and share it with their guests. One good example is the castle cuisine, largely based on age-old recipes, so that guests can 'taste' the Middle Ages in the true sense of the word. The chef, Sam Mahoney, searched ancient manuscripts and books for recipes that went back as far as 1103, the year when Bishop Luffa had the east wing built. He then used them in his culinary creations. He even prepares wonderful dishes on a hay fire...

Amberley Castle lies between the hills of the South Downs and beautiful Wildbrooks and is adjacent to Amberley village, known as the prettiest village in West-Sussex. From here, it is a very short trip to Arundel Castle, Chichester with its historic cathedral and fine houses like Petworth House, Parnham House and Goodwood House, which can all be visited by the public.

The castle offers its guests every possible luxury, and each of the exquisite rooms is named after a castle in Sussex.

Left above and centre: greenery and history combine in the courtyard.

32

Left below: the majestic gatehouse.

34

Joy and Martin Cummings' guests can soak up the atmosphere of the castle

and its inhabitants

through the ages.

06

CHEWTON GLEN

Chewton Glen, New Forest, Christmas Eve 1790. A stiff breeze chases the clouds away and suddenly the moon lights up the cliffs of southern England.
A sailing ship rolls on the waves and a loaded sloop reaches the shore and disembarks. Furtively looking around, dark figures load tobacco, tea and silk, wine and alcohol onto mules and disappear into the woods.
This is an area where smugglers ruled for many years. Until a certain Captain Frederick Marryat kept turning up out of nowhere with his fast ship, the brigantine Rosario, and

broke up the gangs in a very short time. He was an extraordinary man.
In 1817, he made a name for himself as a sailor with the publication of the 'Code of Signals for the Merchant Service', a book about signals and codes for the merchant fleet. In 1821 he portrayed Napoleon on his death bed in St. Helena. In 1824 he was commander of the war ship Larne during the war in Burma. And finally, in 1829, he started his real life's work: writing a series of books full of fantastic tales of the people who sailed the seven seas at that time.
His best-known work was entitled 'Children of the New Forest' and it describes life

vity of two enterprising people: Martin Skan and his Swiss wife Brigitte. They transformed the 19th century manor house, which was built in the Palladian style and is steeped in history, into one of the most exclusive and refined hotels in Great Britain.

When Martin bought Chewton Glen in 1966, it was a small hotel with eight rooms and a single bathroom. Now, it is a paragon of luxury, service and taste, with 35 rooms and 18 suites, beautifully decorated and stylishly furnished, thanks to Brigitte. For this 'Lady of Chewton Glen' has been the driving force behind the tasteful decoration and refurbishment of this English country house, surrounded by 75 acres of landscaped parks with ponds, flower beds, croquet lawns and a breathtakingly beautiful 9-hole golf course.

The red five-star hotel -the only one that is privately owned in Great Britain- has won numerous distinctions in the past few years.

And quite a few of those awards - one of them a Michelin star- were won by Chef Pierre Chevillard, for his wonderful cuisine.

But Chewton Glen has also been highly commended for its impeccable service and its wonderful facilities: the Health Club with its outdoor pool, the Palladian-style indoor pool, one of the most beautiful in Europe, a sauna, whirlpool, Turkish bath, fitness centre and beauty salon, indoor and outdoor tennis. Seven beauty therapists and a tennis coach are at the disposal of the guests.

And if all those facilities are still not enough, you can follow the romantic footpath 'Chewton Bunny' down to the seashore. You can also go fishing, sailing, riding, or sightseeing in the beautiful New Forest area, with gems such as

in the New Forest. He knew the area inside out, for during his wanderings and adventures he stayed on the estate of Chewton Glen, which was owned by his brother.

This is where he wrote his books, and this is where he found his inspiration.

Nowadays, there are many reminders of the captain's stay in the hotel: the bar was named after him; in the hall different items and souvenirs are on show; the suites are named after characters in his books, and the walls are adorned with watercolours, inspired by the sketches he made of his adventures.

But this ode to a sailor would never have come about without the efforts and creati-

Beaulieu, Exbury Gardens, Broadlands, the historic cities of Winchester and Salisbury with their beautiful cathedrals and the fascinating prehistoric Stonehenge. And to make the fairy-tale complete, one more tip: treat yourself to a ride in Chewton Glen's Jaguar,

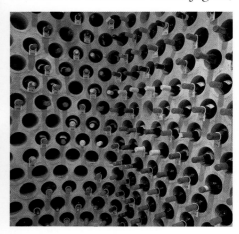

chauffeured by Mr Royston.

He has been showing the 'rich of the world' the beauties of the New Forest for years. He is a living legend, and thanks to him, you will never forget the New Forest – just as you will never forget Chewton Glen.

This Palladian-style manor house
is now one of England's most exclusive hotels.

07

THE LYGON ARMS

A stagecoach with four-in-hand, escorted by heavily-armed horsemen, galloped through the main street of the usually peaceful Broadway in the Cotswolds. With a great deal of noise, the company halted in the village square, which was clouded with dust from the horses' hooves. Stable-boys came running and led the foaming and sweating horses to the stables. Oliver Cromwell descended from the coach and entered The Lygon Arms, which at the time was widely known as The White Hart Inn.

It was the 2nd of September 1651, the day before the Battle of Worcester, which would help bring an end to the civil war that had been ravaging the country for years, and which would change the history of the country forever.

After a last staff meeting with his commanders-in-chief, the landlord led him to the most beautiful room in the inn.

It was a lavishly furnished room, the ceiling of which was decorated with hand-crafted stucco, but Cromwell didn't notice it. Until late at night, he sat there, staring into the fire of the Elizabethan fireplace. His premonition became reality: his army of 'Roundheads' was beaten by the royal troops of Charles I and the King triumphantly led his army through the same Broadway, only to halt... in front of The Lygon Arms.

What better place, after all, to celebrate the victory of his

'Cavaliers' than the very spot where Cromwell had spent the previous night!

For many centuries, The Lygon Arms has been one of the most famous inns in Britain. Broadway's register states that in 1531 the inn was the property of Thomas White, a local wool merchant.

The Lygon Arms actually owes its existence to wool, for in the 14th and 15th centuries the Cotswolds were an important centre of the wool trade and many visiting merchants needed a comfortable place to spend the night.

In the 18th century, the inn became the ideal halting place for coaches which commuted between London and Wales.

Extra stables were built, to house up to 30 horses. In 1820 the estate which contained the inn was bought by William Lygon, a general who had served under Wellington at the

rant and in the winter as a ballroom. This was how 'The Great Hall' came about, the now famous award-winning restaurant of The Lygon Arms.

In the thirties, the hotel became the property of his son Donald, who had inherited his father's love of good food and generous hospitality.

During the Second World War, Donald housed foreign officers, whose memories of their stay must have been unforgettable.

For the contrast between the battlefield and the spartan life at the front, and the peaceful environment of Broadway and the luxury of The Lygon Arms was staggering.

Nowadays, The Lygon Arms is one of the pearls in the crown of the exclusive Savoy group, which guarantees that this precious piece of English heritage and the atmosphere of the time of Cromwell and King Charles will be preserved.

At present, the hotel contains 58 rooms and 5 magnificent suites, divided between the age-old inn and the recent Garden and Orchard wings, which have been

Battle of Waterloo. Before his death, he handed over management of the inn to his butler, Charles Dury. To thank him, Dury changed the name from 'The White Hart Inn' to 'The Lygon Arms'.

In the 19th century, hunting became very popular in the Cotswolds and in order to please the huntsmen who now came to stay in the area, he built a beautiful new hall for their meetings and balls.

Tradition is still kept up at The Lygon Arms: at the beginning of the hunting season, the famous Stirrup Cup is presented here. At the beginning of the 20th century The Lygon Arms was bought by Sydney Bolton Russell.

He intended to restore the slightly neglected inn to its former glory.

He began with the restoration of the old hall, which in the summer served as a restau-

beautifully integrated into the old building. The place is full of antiques and cosy corners with open fires.

The Lygon Arms Country Club offers its guests a beauty centre, sauna, steam room, fitness facilities and a luxurious indoor pool, the roof of which can be opened when the weather is good.

Guests can play billiards, or tennis on the private court, which are reached by way of the well-kept gardens.

Broadway is one of those idyllic villages with houses of honey-coloured stone in the romantic Cotswolds where time has stood still.

The surroundings offer a rich variety of interesting things to see: the imposing Blenheim Castle, Warwick Castle which is one of the most beautiful castles in England; the university town of Oxford with its famous colleges, and of course Shakespeare's birth-place in Stratford-upon-Avon.

A visit to the latter may give you the inspiration to tell your friends and acquaintances the history of The Lygon Arms in just the right words.

THE HEMPEL

It overwhelms and shocks, like the birth of the Renaissance, of Baroque, Art Nouveau or -more recently- Art Deco must have overwhelmed and shocked at the time.

But it never leaves you indifferent. Advocates and opponents heatedly discuss it, expressing feelings and emotions that are hard to express, and hard to understand. This is the final breakthrough of a completely novel approach to architecture, although we laymen are not completely aware of its impact. Luckily, it is an hotel, otherwise it would have to be made into a museum to give people a chance to experience it.

This hotel, this style, simply could not manifest itself before, because the time was not ripe for it.

It is a synthesis of foreign cultures, and the result of the skill to have these interact in exactly the right way, so that they blend into a new architecture, a new style.

Like Roman and Greek art were seeds of the Renaissance and Baroque in the West European field of culture, so Zen culture, Eastern meditation and Oriental simplicity here blend harmoniously into Italian minimalism and Western high-tech. And all this can be found behind an utterly British, bright white, stern façade in nineteenth century middle-class Lancaster Gate, north of Hyde Park.

'More is less' - this is how Anouska Hempel, world-famous architect and owner of the hotel that bears her name, describes her search for minimalism, in which she creates 'Space' with an absolute minimum of lines.

This is London's best hidden jewel. Cab drivers fruitlessly cruise the little streets around Craven Hill Gardens, looking for any sign that says 'Hotel', but the row of bright white Georgian houses gives none of its secrets away... Until an ever-alert gentleman in a modern black suit gestures discreetly and opens an anonymous door.

Through a room full of white orchids, which could be called a 'lock' to another world, you enter the Atrium, an enormous sand-coloured, windowless room with to the left and the right two ever-burning open fires which seem to float. Long Eastern tables, two by each fireplace, are the only objects that break the pattern of lines in the room.

An enormously long stone table, with staff dressed in black, constitutes the reception area: no phones, no computers, no key cabinets or whatever. Light falls through the roof, many floors up, and envelops the reception area and all the corridors on the higher levels in a mysterious, hazy light. Everything exudes peace and quiet.

Going down the translucent glass staircase you reach The Shadow Bar, -the name fits perfectly, for shadows reflect everywhere, and I-Thai, the restaurant.

With its hanging walls and a multi-racial staff selected by Anouska Hempel herself, it serves an original well-balanced combination of Thai, Japanese and Italian high cuisine.

A culinary adventure that has been devised and designed by Anouska Hempel is offered to you by her fantastic, talented young chefs.

The hotel has 44 rooms and 6 suites, all totally different, not just in decoration, but also in lay-out. There are no paintings, drawings or etchings, only figures in white, black and grey. But also squares and circles which have been painted straight onto the walls.

There are orchids everywhere, and here and there objects or antiques from far continents: Chinese hunting chairs, Japanese tables, Chinese trunks.

The bathrooms are in black Belgian granite, with sunken baths, plaster-framed sand-blasted glass and stainless steel, and tap water lit up in the dark by cleverly hidden fibre-optic lighting and a mixture of light and shadow. There are

46

surprises everywhere. But let's go back to the outside world. Just as the 'orchid room' was like a place of transition into the mysterious world of 'Hempel', the private Zen garden square is like another look into the outer world: it has the characteristics of the hotel itself, but is surrounded by the streets of Craven Hill Gardens, and yet is private.

In the middle of the square lawns lie three dark green ponds, surrounded by white gravel, bulbous lime-stones, trumpet trees and immaculately trimmed buxus and taxus hedges and bushes, designer garden furniture of precious teak.

The familiar noises of a metropolis, a London taxi driving his customer into Craven Hill Gardens, not looking for any sign saying 'hotel', but a gentleman in black, gesturing discreetly...

'More is less'

51

09

HOLLINGTON HOUSE

On a bleak winter's afternoon, I pulled open the heavy wooden door of Hollington and left the howling wind and stinging rain behind me, to enter a completely different world.

I stood in the middle of a splendid, oak-panelled room with a monumental fireplace in which a crackling woodfire gave off a wonderful glow. And the icy winter cold was completely forgotten when John Guy welcomed me.

Nestling deep in a cosy armchair, a cup of fragrant coffee close at hand, I listened to his story about the Guy family and

Hollington House.

It started in 1961, when John emigrated to Melbourne in Australia and married Penny. He made his career as a restaurant manager and then managed to purchase Burnham Beeches Estates. He transformed it into one of the most renowned hotels in Australia.

54 But after a number of years the longing for his homeland became too strong and he and his family started to search for a unique property in England, in order to surpass even Burnham Beeches Estate. It took several years before they found what they were looking for: Hollington House, a beautiful country house on the border between Hampshire and Berkshire, built in 1904 by E. Festus Kelly, founder of 'Kelly's Directory'.

Mr. Kelly was an ambitious man and he commissioned no lesser person than Arthur Conran Blomfield, an architect with extremely impressive credentials, who had designed everything from castles, such as that of the Baron and Duchess of Bessborourgh, to Barclays Bank in Fleet Street, London. He was even employed on several occasions by His Royal Highness the Prince of Wales.

For the landscaping of the gardens in 1908, he called on Gertrude Jekyll no less, one of the most famous garden designers ever.

In 1921 the whole estate, which then comprised 2,500 acres, went to Eliot Cohen, a millionaire who was, amongst other things, owner of the Lewis Department Stores chain. And in 1991 it was John Guy's turn: a challenge he and his family enthusiastically took on.

With the help of Janet Napier, the female gardener who has been looking after the garden for 22 years, hundreds of rhododendrons were brought over from the Netherlands. The

Edwardian style house contains 20 luxurious rooms with extremely spacious bathrooms, each with its own name and theme.

In the cosy, wood-panelled restaurant the chef presents his star cuisine. In 1995 the hotel won the 'New World Wine Cellar of the Year' award. Need we say more?

When John Guy ran his restaurants in Australia, he acquired a passion for local Australian wines, and in a short time, he built up a wine collection of more than 1000 bins.

His passion remained with him on his return to England. For wine lovers, Hollington House not only offers a wide range of European wines, but also the chance to discover Australia as a wine country.

The wine-list gives some interesting information about the various wine-growers and the Australian area from which the wine originates. He is so passionate about the subject that he even organises wine evenings at Hollington House and sometimes he even invites wine-growers all the way from Australia!

Hollington House is situated in an area classified as an 'Area of Outstanding Natural Beauty'.

The terrace offers a wonderful view of the towers and flag-poles of Highclere Castle, home of Lord Carnarvon, Horse racing manager for the Queen.

The castle, which is open to the public, is certainly worth visiting. It was designed by Sir Charles Barry, architect of the Houses of Parliament in London, and it contains a wonderful collection of Egyptian treasures. The Fifth Earl of Carnarvon, the Lord's grandfather, discovered the tomb of Tutankhamen.

Another reason to stay at Hollington House for a couple of days...

Relaxing in an easy chair by the open fire,
I listened to the story.

10

THE CHESTER GROSVENOR

This is not just the story of an hotel, but also of a town, of a country and... of one of the most powerful and aristocratic families in England.

The first Grosvenor ancestor who set foot on English soil was no less than the commander of the troops of William the Conqueror.

Later, in the Middle Ages, they fought as Crusaders in the Holy Land, stood alongside the royalists during the Civil war and served their country in battles against Napoleon and during both World Wars.

For its countless services to its country, the family was rewarded in 1874 with the title of 'Duke of Westminster'. Nowadays, Gerald Grosvenor, 6th Duke of Westminster and an intimate friend of the Prince of Wales, reigns over a world-wide empire, ranging from real estate in the exclusive areas of Mayfair and Belgravia, through dozens of landed estates spread across three continents. Moreover, he is the owner of the American embassy in London, the only embassy that does not belong to the United States.

One of the jewels in his crown is the Chester Grosvenor Hotel, not only because of the splendour of the estate, but also because of its age-old history, so closely related to the past of his own family.

Let us go back to the 17th century. The 'Golden Talbot' was an inn, just inside the walls of the mighty town of Chester. Merchants and travellers, tired after their long journey, reached the town via the east gate and were immediately tempted by the cosiness of the tavern, where a good meal and a soft bed awaited them.

But the inn also knew bad times: famine, plague and war. Chester, a bastion of the royalists during the Civil war, was invaded and besieged by Cromwell's troops and the 'Golden Talbot' received a direct hit and was almost completely destroyed.

But the inn rose from its ashes time and again. At the end of the 18th century and the beginning of the 19th century, it became a veritable luxury hotel, under the name 'Royal Hotel'.

For twenty-eight years, the Royal Hotel housed the head-quarters of the Independent Party, a political party which spoke out against the Grosvenor dynasty.

The party got its come-uppance when Count Grosvenor went behind the backs of his political opponents and bought the building, forcing them to find other premises.

This is how the hotel became the property of one of the most famous families in England, and a monument in the social life of high society at the time.

In the middle of the 19th century, the number of guests at the Royal Hotel grew in proportion to the expansion of Britain's world empire under Queen Victoria.

There came a moment when the hotel could no longer handle the amount of people wanting to stay there. The building was pulled down and a magnificent, imposing hotel was erected in its place: 'The Chester Grosvenor'.

The greatest highlight for the new hotel was when Edward, Prince of Wales and future king, came to stay for three days in 1869. While the band of the Artillery Volunteers played 'God save the Prince of Wales', Lady Grosvenor led him into the beautifully decorated hotel, where he occupied a suite consisting of eight rooms.

If there is a secret to the success of the Grosvenor empire, it lies in the family motto 'Virtue, not Ancestry'.

The family did not trade on its ancestry, but kept looking towards the future.

This becomes clear in the plans made for 'The Chester Grosvenor'.

Although the hotel was still a paragon of good taste and tradition, it was beginning to look its venerable age.

Under the management of Jonathan Slater, considerable restoration work was undertaken. Each room was allotted a

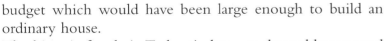

budget which would have been large enough to build an ordinary house.

The historic façade in Tudor timber was throughly renewed as well. The result was a building of the most magnificent luxury.

Chester is one of the most beautiful towns in England, completely walled in and renowned for its unique 'rows' - the 13th century galleries or arcades on the ground and first floors of the houses, which allowed people to shop and go to inns under cover.

These pedestrian areas consist of wooden or stone pillars with half-timbered arches. This special feature can also be found in the façade of The Chester Grosvenor.

Walking and shopping in medieval surroundings, without getting wet: the ultimate luxury even continues outside the walls of The Chester Grosvenor.

GIDLEIGH PARK

Who, as a child, has never dreamed of discovering a fairy-tale land, somewhere behind high mountains or, when wandering in the woods, behind mysterious gates that open suddenly?

Well, it happened to me, and I'm a grown-up with my feet firmly on the ground.

It started when I drove into the village of Chagford: the houses, the little church, the market square seemed to be made of gingerbread, marzipan, sugar and chocolate.

But that other world did not reveal its secrets all that easily. It was as if only a lost traveller could be granted the privilege of discovering it 'by accident'. I found my way through a maze of ever-narrower hedges and walled-in paths. The journey continued through tunnels of green and along narrow roads that rose and fell to the rhythm of the rolling landscape.

Miniature stone bridges over rustling streams helped me reach the other side of one small valley after another.

This was no longer a human-sized world. And when I gradually began to wonder where the gnomes and the elves might be, the narrow road ended in a hidden glade and the wild landscape imperceptibly changed into a glorious park through which a murmuring river flowed.

And right at the end of this fairy-tale valley, leaning against a wall of hills, stood the ultimate discovery: the Xanadu of Kay and Paul Henderson, a breathtakingly beautiful and romantic manor house in mock Tudor style.

This American couple, who had no experience at all of hotel management, bought Gidleigh Park in 1977.

The wonderful house was built in 1929 by an Australian shipping magnate and is now one of the pearls in the crown of the English hotel world.

The tranquility, cosiness and intimacy of the surroundings finds its way inside, through the hall and the wide-open windows at the side of the terrace. Siamese cats lie purring by the ever-burning open fire.

The bar, the restaurant and many of the rooms enjoy an incomparable view of the wonderful surroundings.

Everywhere, beautiful bouquets and plentiful baskets of fruit reflect the perfect refinement of the place. The kitchen is just as wonderful: the young,

talented chef Michael Caines trained under no less than Raymond Blanc in England and Bernard Loiseau and Joël Robuchon in France.

The wine list offers a wide selection, but a large section is devoted to the best Californian wines -proof of Paul Henderson's love for his country and heritage.

My stay at Gidleigh Park is a short one, unfortunately, so for my predinner drink, I choose the most strategic place to savour the atmosphere: the idyllic terrace.

I sit in front of the lovely white façade with its carved wood ornamentation and while I enjoy the wonderful delicacies of the chef which accompany my cocktail, I look out over the 'Garden of Eden' below.

My glance falls on the small North Teigh river that sends its clear water from the hills of Dartmoor through the garden over a bed of moss-covered rocks. And beyond the lawns and the flower beds, just visible between the greenery, stands a cottage with a thatched roof.

The Hendersons made two suites in this dream house, next to the green carpet, softer than the baize of a snooker table,

that is the croquet lawn.

The name 'Gidleigh' stems from the Middle Ages and is derived from Gidda, the name of the mother of King Harold IIth, who owned the property at the time.

Gidleigh Park is in Dartmoor, the largest National Park in the South of England and a place of many myths and legends.

It borders on Cornwall, home of the legendary King Arthur and Merlin the Magician.

This is the mysterious 'land of elves', full of prehistoric reli- gious stones and once, long ago, a bastion of the Celtic and Saxon druids.

Everything is so beautiful here that I have to keep pinching myself to make sure I'm not dreaming.

It is time to go, and I remember a story from my childhood, about a little boy who always carried a bag of pebbles.

Every now and then he dropped one, to leave a trail and not get lost in the woods. For I worry that when I wake up tomorrow, this will all be a dream and I will never be able to find this fairytale land again.

The beauty
and poetry of the surroundings
can be felt inside the house.

12

THE DEVONSHIRE ARMS & COUNTRY CLUB

"When the governors of Chatsworth took over the running of the hotel, which had been the property of our family since 1753, the chairman of the board, the Marquess of Harington, asked me to take on the interior decoration and the furnishing. I was very pleased to accept the task.

They intended to make The Devonshire Arms into an hotel with the atmosphere of a country house.

I have tried to achieve this by having furniture, paintings, etchings and drawings sent from Chatsworth, our manor house in Derbyshire.

I used these priceless antiques to decorate the public rooms and the bedrooms in the old part of the hotel.

This has now been harmoniously integrated into a building that has been an inn since the 17th century.

In 1982, the Wharfedale wing was built on, and now The Devonshire Arms has 41 guest rooms, many with four-poster beds made by our own carpenters from Chatsworth, and filled with souvenirs from our own family. In the Park Top room, for example, the silks can be seen that were worn by jockey Lester Piggot when he won the world famous King George VI and Queen Elizabeth Stakes at Ascot, riding the Queen's horse, Park Top.

The carpet depicting a sheep in the Shepherd's room was created by my daughter.

This room, by the way, contains other souvenirs of the shepherd's tradition in this part of Yorkshire. And the Crace Room is decorated in the

style of the well-known 19th-century interior designer Crace; the wallpaper is a reproduction of a drawing by Mr Crace.

Also, if you look carefully, you will notice that many rooms have a stylised snake woven into their carpets - the symbol of our Devonshire family. Our Chef, Andrew Nicholson, can be considered one of the most reputed culinary masters in Yorkshire. He uses an abundance of fish and game from the estate, and fresh vegetables from our own garden.

The English Automobile Association has awarded him two well-earned Rosettes for the superior quality of the food. The Georgian-style restaurant 'The Burlington' is adorned with reproductions and drawings by William Kent, a friend and colleague of the Count of Burlington, one of our ancestors.

In the 17th-century stables opposite the hotel we have installed a comprehensive beauty and fitness centre, with heated pool, jacuzzi, steam room, solarium and fitness room. A trained team of therapists stands by to give aromatherapy and other treatments and massages using the most advanced methods.

Light lunches can be taken in the lounge near the pool and barbecues are regularly organised on the patio.

Everybody who comes to Wharfdale for the first time, is rendered speechless by the beauty of the landscape here.

On our vast Bolton Abbey Estate, in the middle of the Yorkshire Dales National Park, you can stroll along the river towards the ruins of Bolton Priory, through woods and heathland. A number of activities are organised from The Devonshire Arms: falcon hunting, a six thousand year old sport; fishing on the Wharfe river, which runs for six miles through the Bolton Abbey Estate, and golfing at the nearby Skipton Golf Club in the beautiful surroundings of the Yorkshire Dales.

'Northern Exposure' is a colourful introduction to rural life in Yorkshire. The guests start the day with a guided tour of a local farm where old farming methods are still used, followed by a sightseeing trip in the area by four-wheel drive car. After a meal at a local farm, a guide shows them the most important historic and scenic sights of the area.

For a touch of nostalgia, guests who want to see the area in an original way can make use of a convertible vintage sports car.

Our family are proud of Chatsworth Castle, which is considered to be one of the most valuable manor houses in England. It is a very special feeling to have a gem like The Devonshire Arms as part of one's heritage...″

Deborah Devonshire, Duchess of Devonshire

69

Everywhere you look there are fine antiques, paintings, etchings and souvenirs from world-famous Chatsworth Castle, also owned by the family.

13

TYLNEY HALL

On the border between the counties of Berkshire and Hampshire, no more than an hour's drive from Londen, lies a 66 acre estate of landscaped gardens with a wealth of age-old trees.

The stately grounds form a splendid background for the impressive Tylney Hall.

Although an inscription on the grave of Frederick Tylney indicates that a manor house has stood here since 1561, proof did not materialise until 1774, in the form of a map which shows that the Tylney family possessed a large domain that comprised of various parishes and villages and stretched far beyond Odiham.

Frederick, the last male Tylney, died in 1725 and the property was inherited by his niece, who was married to the later Baron of Tylney.

One of the later residents, the fifth Baron of Mornington, had Tylney Hall as it was then, completely pulled down for the price of the scrap material and the wood. In 1898 Lionel Phillips bought the estate for £ 77,000.

He made Tylney Hall the impressive estate it still is today.

Although everything dates from the turn of the century, it gives the impression of being much older.

The ceiling of the 'Smoking Room' was copied from a 16th century example, but the crowning glory is the 'Great Hall', partly clad in Italian walnut. A wonderful stone fireplace, and an Italian ceiling brought over from the Grimation Palace in Florence, make for impressive public areas.

During World War I, Tylney Hall was used as a hospital, after which Lord Rotherwick became its next owner.

He was a high-ranking Cavalry Officer of great merit as well as a succesful businessman. During World War II, Tylney Hall became the head office for his shipping company, the well-known Clan Shipping Line.

In 1985, after many changes in its long history, Tylney Hall reached its final purpose, as a luxury hotel with an authentic English country house atmosphere.

It is a wonderful experience to take a stroll through the grounds, from where the graceful façades can be seen constantly. Return to the Library Bar to enjoy a gin and tonic, or a cocktail.

The crackle of bruning wood from the open fireplace in the Italian Lounge is the only interruption while you peruse the A La Carte menu and the extensive Wine list.

Dinner is served in the magnificent glass-domed Oak Room Restaurant.

The vast estate is situated adjacent to an 18-hole golf course and guests can enjoy many activities: clay pigeon shooting, archery, falconry and horse riding.

Trips in a hot air balloon can also be organised with prior notice.

The surrounding countryside is every bit as fascinating and steeped in history as Tylney Hall itself.

A short distance from the estate there are many interesting manor houses and castles to be visited, such as The Vyne, a Tudor manor surrounded by a beautifully landscaped garden. Or try driving to the south west, through the rolling landscape of the South Downs and the Micheldever Forest to Winchester.

This former capital of England has a stunning Norman cathedral and a medieval centre that is certainly worth a visit.

Close by are the historic towns of Guildford and Reading. Also the towns of Odiham and Farnham are not to be missed.

The hotel offers excellent gym and sauna facilities, with the option of indoor and outdoor swimming pools.

The magnificent suites and master suites offer rooms from a bygone era. Each have splendid views of the carefully kept gardens and ponds.

Some have four poster beds and jacuzzi baths. Separate cottage bedrooms are found in the original kitchen gardens, whose splendour is being restored.

Tylney Hall
dates from around the turn of the century,
but everything seems much older here.

Above: the 'Oak Room' restaurant
Centre: the 'Great Hall'
Right Below: the 'Drawing Room'

Right page, Above:
still life in the restaurant and in one of the rooms.
Below: the Italian Lounge and the Library Bar.

CHARLTON HOUSE

The road of life can be strange, fascinating and full of surprises. Would Roger Saul ever have thought, all those years ago, when he, as a twenty-one year old, with a starting capital of £500, designed his first leather belt, that one day, having built an empire worth millions, he would find a new challenge and a new passion in creating Charlton House, a unique hotel of incredible refinement?

Roger Saul grew up not far from Shepton Mallet, an unremarkable little town in Somerset, south of historic Bath and Wells. And although, as a young man, he was determined to make his mark on the world, he remained fascinated by a mysterious, centuries-old manor house, mentioned in the great Domesday survey and situated in the middle of a wonderful park on the banks of the river Sheppey. When he was a child, the rich citizens and the local noblemen held wedding parties there, and other celebrations.

Twenty-five years ago, in this small provincial town, the star of the Mulberry empire started to rise. With the ultimate refinement and good taste of a man who appreciates the good things in life, Saul created leather goods and country-style clothes for both ladies and men.

Mulberry shops sprang up all over the world and Roger Saul insisted on personally decorating each of these shops with antiques, materials and objects of the very highest quality. And because more and more customers asked for: 'this standard lamp and that cushion' of 'that side table' or 'the settee over there', objects that were part of the shop and not for sale, Roger decided to start designing furniture and decorative pieces for the home - which would later become his famous 'Home Collection'. A wonderful idea which turned out to be very lucrative.

In the meantime, Roger had moved into his new headquarters, Kilver Court, a 15th-century manor house with magnificent gardens.

But there was one problem: where in Shepton Mallet could he find accommodation for the many suppliers, clients and other visitors to Mulberry?

It was then that Roger remembered the manor house by the river. Soon, everything had been arranged and architects, builders, carpenters and the creative team of Mulberry started work.

Roger and his wife Monty scoured auctions, antique fairs and antique shops all over Europe - and the result is breathtaking.

This masterpiece can best be defined as a 'home' - referring to the very British difference between a 'house' and a 'home'. And although officially it was Roger Ames who had Charlton House built in 1630 for his bride, the book 'Buildings of England' by the well-known architect Nicolaus Pevsner tells that a house on that spot was mentioned in the Domesday book in the 11th century. Moreover, the author refers to an Elizabethan façade, which would have been built between 1558 and 1603. But the eastern façade is the oldest, with windows that date from the time of Henry VIII. Other windows and a magnificent fireplace that still adorns the hall, are Jacobean.

It is generally assumed that Roger Ames bought an existing building and, like every generation of the Ames family after him, renovated and expanded it extensively.

In 1804, the estate came into the hands of the Wickham family.

They had the road re-routed to allow the house more space, added a Georgian façade and created a wonderful park with an ornamental pond. As we said before, Roger Saul bought a house in which the atmosphere of the many parties that had been held there still lingered. He improved Charlton House even more, furnishing it with his most beautiful Mulberry creations - a marriage between joie de vivre and good taste.

The concept of 'marriage' on the one hand, and the manor house on the other hand, are united forever: the day after the opening the new Charlton House hotel hosted a wedding party where 180 guests took their place at the dinner table. And the finest of the 17 beautifully decorated rooms is the bridal suite, which features a four-poster bed with figures of Adam and Eve carved into the beautiful wood and with secret cupboards in the headboard.

The centuries-old coat of arms of the Ames family still symbolises the atmosphere of Charlton House: a wedding ring and a rose.

At Charlton House,
the Mulberry creations make
the difference between
'house' and 'home'.

THE STAFFORD

A squadron of Royal Air Force bombers triumphantly flew in formation over the exclusive St. James area of London.

Far below, in a courtyard, hidden behind the stately façade of the most renowned of London's Gentlemen's Clubs, the music of the Andrews Sisters emanated from the crowded bar.

Exhiliarated American and Canadian officers were celebrating, for the end of World War II was near and they would soon be on their way home. They said goodbye to each other and to the bartender of their 'American Club'.

During those war years, this cosy pub had been their 'home' and they did not want to go without leaving a souvenir.

That is why a wonderful surprise awaits guests at the Stafford Hotel, when they enter this unique hotel bar.

From the ceiling hang hundreds of ties, model airplanes and ships.

The walls are completely covered in photographs, from aircraft carriers to fighters, and the signatures of famous peop-

le. The tradition of leaving mementos continues to the present day. This legendary bar is a testimony to one of the most fascinating episodes in the history of The Stafford.

'Number 17, St. James's Place' was built in the 18th century and was once the residence of Lord and Lady Lyttleton.

In 1849 Lady Lyttleton, grand-daughter of Lord Spencer, an ancestor of Diana, Princess of Wales, was appointed governess to the children of Queen Victoria.

This meant they had to move and they put 'Number 17' up for sale.

In the following years, it housed some of the most selective gentlemen's clubs and private hotels - the 'Richmond Club Chambers', the 'Green's Private Hotel' and the 'St. James Hotel', to which the 'Stafford Club' was added in 1886. In 1912 the house, together with 'Number 16' and 'Number 18' became the Stafford Hotel.

The present owners, a private British company, bought the hotel in 1995.

They were fascinated by its legendary history, its atmosphere and its tradition of a typical English club, and attracted by the exclusive St. James area between Piccadilly and Green Park.

The Stafford Hotel had by this time also acquired the adjoining 18th-century stables, the 'Carriage House', which could accommodate 12 luxurious rooms. It looked out on a romantic courtyard, the 'Blue Ball Yard'.

The building was originally stables built by Lord Godolphin, who lived in a grand house in St James's.

The Carriage House rooms are above the 350-year-old wine cellars. These became the property of a London wine merchant in 1880, whose sign still hangs there!

Here, Gino Nardella, wine expert of 'The Stafford' rules over a priceless wine collection of 18,000 to 20,000 bottles. According to Gino, the hotel stocks some 800 different kinds of wine, 400 of which can be found on the wine list of the restaurant.

The remainder is maturing in the cellars. In spare moments, Gino loves taking guests down to his beloved cellars. Even here, the 'Club' tradition continues. It is a favourite venue of London aristocracy, used for private meetings and candle-lit dinners amongst the thousands of wine bottles.

With its very personal style and service, The Stafford has managed to preserve the atmosphere of a private house or club. The whole hotel has recently been renovated, and all 80 rooms and suites have airconditioning. They are stylishly upholstered and furnished in mahogany, chintz and Irish linen, each different from the other, and all the bathrooms have been refurbished in gleaming black and white

marble. The cuisine, too, is of exceptional quality, prepared by Chris Oakes, a much awarded English gourmet chef and his 14 assistants.

The lounge is a wonderful place to have afternoon tea and soak up the atmosphere.

At the end of the day, pay a visit to the busy, convivial 'American Bar', and enjoy the nostalgic atmosphere of days gone by.

It is as if nothing has changed since the days when London's most exclusive Gentlemen's Club was housed here.

16

LUCKNAM PARK

He pulled aside the heavy, lace-edged curtain to get a better view of the majestic Beech tree avenue that stretched from the house for almost a mile.

The first carriages came up the driveway and halted in front of the Palladian columns of Lucknam Park.

Liveried servants helped the grand ladies and gentlemen out of the carriages, and he Andreas Christian Boode, hurried down-stairs to greet his guests.

Sir Andreas was the son of a Dutchman who had owned some five coffee plantations in the tro-pics. It was a very special day in 1834, Andreas was honouring his brilliant and well travelled son John who had just married Clementina.

Eight hundred guests travelled from all over the country to join the spectacular celebrations.

A salvo of cannon shots signalled the start of an extravagent feast set out in the grounds of the house. An artists impression of the day can be seen today in the hotel's reception area.

The newly weds had four daugh-ters, two of whom died young. Years later, the couple divorced and Clementina left both her hus-band with their two daughters. The interior of the house was much altered at this time. The hall was panelled in dark oak, with carved beams, and coats of arms on the ceiling.

There was a large library in the now drawing room. The present restaurant was a conservatory.

Soon after Sir John's death in 1870 the estate was sold.

The house has been traced to before the Norman conquest of 1066, the name Lucknam Park, referring to a Saxon settlement. From as far back as 1199 to 1688 there was a farmhouse on the current site of the hotel.

The Boode family were one of several wealthy merchant families who lived at Lucknam Park between 1688 and 1987. Then the house was bought and converted into a luxurious hotel with excellent facilities set amidst 500 acres of listed parkland.

Today the award winning hotel has gained a reputation for being amongst the finest in the country.

Set only six miles from the Georgian city of Bath, the location offers the perfect opportunity to explore the city, visiting the numerous historical sites, museums and the numerous individual shops.

Guests searching for a more reclusive stay can happily spend their time never setting foot outside the estate.

Several hundred yards from the house is one of the most renowned equestrian centres in the United Kingdom from where guests can explore the estate on horseback.

It is managed by Richard Mills, who for six years was responsible for the horses and stables of HRH, The Prince of Wales at Highgrove.

From the central courtyard, with its manicured green lawn, an almost secret passage leads to a splendid tropical inspired garden and to the Leisure Spa.

A beautiful pavilion built in neo-classical style, this spa is a

haven for relaxation and exercise. There is an indoor heated pool, whirlpool, sauna, steam room and solarium.

At the hotel's Beauty Salon, treatments are given using Clarins and Matis skincare products.

Physical and mental stress can be soothed away using relaxing oils, revitalising algae and mud baths.

Everything in this hotel exudes refinement. Each of the eleven suites and thirty one rooms are decorated with wonderful fabrics in rich colours and exquisite antiques are everywhere.

All the bedrooms have marble bathrooms and a breathtaking view of the gardens or the parkland.

The restaurant has been awarded some of the highest culinary accolades and is supported by a wine list of 400 labels, many unique, produced by small growers.

Whether you are reclining in the Drawing Room, Library or dining in the Main Restaurant, with its magnificent handpainted ceiling and crystal chandeliers –you will feel as welcome and privileged as a guest of Sir Andreas Boode and his son Sir John.

17

MAISON TALBOOTH

He was sitting on a folding chair in a clearing in the wooded hills, his painter's palette in his left hand.

His paintbrush, held loosely in his right hand, made masterly strokes on the canvas. Every now and then, he stopped for minutes at a time and let his glance fall on the idyllic valley beneath him.

The panorama was bucolic: a river flowed through the fields and passed a romantic house on the banks, to disappear finally under a moss-covered stone bridge.

On the horizon, the little church of Dedham rose above the small huddle of houses. The sound of its bells filled the valley - just about the only touch of beauty that could not be found in his painting.

It was a masterpiece, and he proudly signed his name, 'John Constable', the most renowned English landscape painter of all times.

Now, a hundred years later, the painting takes pride of place in the National Gallery of Scotland.

The clearing on the hill is deserted now, apart from a young deer grazing, but the house on the river is humming with life.

The terrace, between the white façade with its decorative wood carvings and the gently flowing river, is filled with tables where people sit enjoying the view.

With a flourish, waiters serve the most exquisite dishes, and serve wonderful French wines.

Inside, in the busy restaurant, the atmosphere is just as cosy. The maitre comments on the menu with its graceful heading 'Le Talbooth Restaurant' and Gerald Milsom and his son Paul give discreet instructions to the staff. Gerald can be proud of what he has achieved here.

As a the founder of Pride of Britain, a group of stylish romantic country house hotels in the United Kingdom, he knows the business inside out.

In 1952 he bought the delapidated Tudor house on the river. Its history goes back to the beginning of the 16th century and the name 'Talbooth' stems from 1786, when there was a toll bridge on the spot where the road to Ipswich crossed the river Stour.

Even the boats that sailed this idyllic waterway had to pay.

'Le Talbooth' became widely renowned for its excellent cuisine and its beautiful location - so much so that Gerald had to expand the existing house.

More and more visitors were sorry to have to leave Constable Country so soon after a wonderful meal. That is why Gerald Milsom bought a magnificent Victorian manor house, painted a pastel pink, with a view of Dedham valley and the medieval church of Stratford St. Mary.

It stood half a mile further on, on a softly rolling grassy hill. He called it Maison Talbooth, and he made it into an hotel. On first impression, both the outside and the interior remind one of a refined private home.

In the hall, guests sign the enormous, heavy visitor's book, and are then taken to the spacious guest rooms, each named after an English poet.

Everything breathes luxury: some rooms have their own sitting room and two of them feature round, sunken baths.

A copious breakfast is served in the room, for the house con-

93

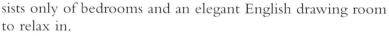

sists only of bedrooms and an elegant English drawing room to relax in.

Half a mile away, in the restaurant, the dining tables are set and a gastronomic meal with French and English dishes is prepared.

The walk there is wonderful, but there is always a chauffeur-driven car on hand to take you there.

This is rural East Anglia, north of London, with its small fairy-tale villages, which owe their existence to the wealth engendered by the medieval wool trade with Flanders.

Many noble families in the area still own the manor houses and castles of their ancestors.

The town of Colchester, with its history that goes back to Roman time, is close by.

An excursion to Cambridge, the historic university town with its many colleges, is an absolute must, and London is within easy reach.

You can go and see all that beauty on canvas at the Victoria and Albert Museum, or at the Tate Gallery, where John Constable's works have been -and will remain- 'guests of honour' for a long time.

Back at Maison Talbooth, you can take a guided drive or walk through Constable Country, and be brought to the afo-rementioned clearing in the wooded hills, and see that nothing has changed in the past hundred years.

This heavenly spot seems as eternal as the painting itself. In the valley below, the bells of Dedham church are ringing.

18

THORNBURY CASTLE

"When I came hither I was Lord High Constable
And Duke of Buckingham; now, poor Edward Bohun.
Yet I am richer than my base accusers
That never knew what truth meant..."
(from 'Henry VIII' by Shakespeare)

After these pathetic words Edward Stafford, the Third Duke of Buckingham, betrayed by false testimonies by his servants and recently condemned to death, left Westminster Hall and climbed the scaffold.

These events were a dramatic climax to the turbulent history of Thornbury Castle.

The 'Manor of Thornbury' can be traced back to the reign of King Athelstan (925-940 A.D.).

Later, William the Conquerer, no less, took possession of Thornbury, which at the time was owned by a certain Britvic, and gave the estate as a gift to his wife, Queen Matilda.

There were rumours that Matilda, before she got engaged to William, had met Britvic at the house of her father, Boudewijn, Count of Flanders; that she had fallen madly in love with him and had proposed marriage several times.

But he rejected her and she sought revenge.

When William embarked on his war of conquest in England, she managed to persuade her husband to take Thornbury from Britvic and the poor man spent the rest of his days in the dungeon at Winchester.

The manor and castle of Thornbury was eventually given by the

King to Robert Fitzhamon whom he also made the 1st Earl of Gloucester.

The property remained in the hands of their descendants until it passed by marriage in the 14th century to Ralph the 2nd Earl of Stafford.

It was this Earl's grandson who married the last Plantagenet princess, the grand-daughter of Edward III.

Their marriage produced a son who became the 1st Duke of Buckingham.

The 2nd Duke of Buckingham was executed by Richard III when he was 27 years old and the estates passed to his son Edward III, Duke of Buckingham.

Thus began the story which was so lyrically described by Shakespeare. In 1510, King Henry VIII gave Edward permission to build a new castle, right next to the old existing manor. Up to this day, the date 1511 can be read on the gatehouse.

It became one of the largest and most talked about building projects of its time: a magnificent castle with a large hall, chapel, store room, wine cellar, kitchens, bedrooms, hermitage, prison and a beautiful courtyard.

Around that time, a new building style, typical of the Renaissance, came into existence.

Reinforced strongholds, meant to resist sieges, made way for manor houses which were reinforced to a degree by battlements, loop-holes and turrets. Gradually, the purpose of these became mainly decorative.

With the appearance of the cannon, wars were fought mainly on the battlefield instead of by conquering castles, so these strongholds became superfluous.

However, once the building of the mighty Thornbury Castle was in progress, it became clear that the castle had been conceived in such a way that it could easily become a military bastion.

That was not what Henry VIII had in mind when he gave permission for the building.

The King considered Thornbury to be a real threat to his crown, and this, together with the royal airs and graces assumed by the Third Duke of Buckingham and the false accusations of his servant, induced Henry VIII to accuse him of high treason, with all the aforesaid consequences. After his death, the unfinished castle was confiscated by the King.

Queen Mary Tudor spent part of her childhood there and Henry VIII stayed there for a while with Ann Boleyn.

Later, Thornbury was returned to the Stafford heirs, but they were financially unable to restore the castle to its former splendour, let alone finish it according to the original plans.

It disintegrated into a wonderful ruin. In 1727, the Howards, Dukes of Norfolk, came into the estate by marriage.

In the middle of the nineteenth century Anthony Salvin started the daunting restoration work. Thornbury finally became what it should have been in the sixteenth century: a splendid residence, worthy of its unfortunate founder, the Third Duke of Buckingham.

Its present owners, the Baron and Baroness of Portlethen, continue the great task.

And how better to honour the Duke than by transforming this breathtaking piece of history into a luxury hotel where guests can enjoy the pomp and splendour of the past?

The hotel has luxurious rooms with four poster beds and glowing open fires, and serves delicious meals in three intimate restaurants, full of wall hangings, coats of arms and Tudor fireplaces.

Thornbury Castle, north of Bristol and Bath and not far from beautiful Wales, is surrounded by 15 acres, has the oldest Tudor garden in England and even boasts a vineyard, which yields enough delicious house wine to survive many years of occupation.

99

19

HUNSTRETE HOUSE

If you want to soak up the cosy atmosphere of the English country nobility, Hunstrete House is the place to be. Hunstrete is not like an hotel at all, it is more like an exquisite manor house with a drawing room, a library and a dining room furnished with beautiful antiques, paintings and china collections.

The warm family atmosphere is particularly enjoyable when, in winter, after a day's walking in the countryside or a visit to nearby historic cities like Bristol, Wells or the Roman spa of Bath, you sit warming yourself at one of the open fireplaces.

'Houndstreet Estate' dates from 963 A.D., when King Athelstan donated it to Glastonbury Abbey.

After 1130, it was let to a local nobleman for the price of ten salmon a year!

When the abbey had disappeared, the estate came into private hands, and it was in the possession of the Popham family of Littlecote for more than three centuries.

During the Civil War, the sons of the family were ardent supporters of Parliament and Colonel Alexander Popham was one of the commanders of the western troops who fought the royal armies.

Just in time, he took the side of the royalists and he helped King Charles II back onto the throne.

This prevented Hunstrete from being totally destroyed, and the estate remained in the family.

Not a trace is left of the house that the monks of Glastonbury built, but Hunstrete House as it is now goes back to the beginning of the 17th century, even though most of it is in Georgian style.

A legend tells that once, an enemy of the family pronounced a curse that the male lineof the Pophams would beco-

me extinct. And believe it or not, his prediction came true: twice Hunstrete has passed on to maternal cousins.

The first time this happened Major General Leyborne took the name of 'Popham' and integrated his own coat of arms with that of the Pophams. This can still be seen in the stone-hewn coat of arms over the main entrance.

The last Popham sold the castle in 1956. The entire estate comprises about 92 acres, 6 acres of which are intensively cultivated. The rest contains deer parks, meadows and woods and even a river. Hunstrete House is now under the ownership of the Fentum family.

Hunstrete House is an exceptional hotel in more ways than one. For instance, as you stroll around the grounds, you will suddenly come upon the 'Ice House' a 20-foot deep cellar which was once used as a freezer. During the winter, vast blocks of ice were hacked from the lake nearby and stacked in the cellars. Slaughtered animals were placed inside and frozen for an indeterminate length of time.

The gardens which are surrounded by Victorian walls and

the vegetable gardens supply the hotel kitchen with all kinds of vegetables and fruit. In 1991, after years of intensive cultivation, the first kiwis were picked!

Bright green, well-kept lawns, where croquet is played, surround the House and are bordered by wonderfully colourful flower beds. By the way, fresh flowers are picked every day and arranged into attractive bouquets to adorn the reception rooms and guest rooms. Out of season, plants and flowers are grown in the greenhouses and dried.

In short: Hunstrete House is its own purveyor by appointment and it is very rare that any vegetables, fruit of flowers have to be brought in from outside.

You can sample the wonderful cuisine on a summer's evening in the courtyard, where once the horse-drawn coaches arrived. You will be surrounded by a wealth of flowers which wind themselves upwards along the ancient walls, and when you inhale their wonderful scents, you will wonder whether you are in England or in France. Wherever it is, this is a very special place.

20

STAPLEFORD PARK

Imagine the scene – the drawing room of Buckingham Palace at the end of the 19th century.

Queen Victoria and Crown Prince Edward sat alone in front of the fire, the former proud and cold, her son sulking.

For some time now the young prince had been looking for a residence worthy of his position, but his search from Cornwall to the Highlands of Scotland had come to nothing. That is, not until a few days earlier, when a friend had mentioned an impressive but discreet estate in the county of Leicestershire, Middle England.

After hurrying there and finding his dream home, there was only one thing left to do – persuade his mother to pay the bill.

Sadly, Stapleford's reputation went before him and wild stories of debauched hunting parties did nothing to impress the Queen.

Stapleford was not quite as discreet as she would have liked and she chose the slightly more staid Sandringham.

In 1894 Stapleford became the property of the Lord John

adventure, for behind every door a new surprise awaits. Twenty-five famous interior designers each furnished a room in their distinctive style: Nina Campbell, Wedgewood, Lady Jane Churchill and David Hicks to name but a few. Equally original are the rooms in the cottage, all of which have been sponsored by famous brand names such as IBM, Coca Cola, MGM and Range Rover, and are furnished in each company's classic style. It is not difficult to guess what hangs on the walls of the Pirelli room, and we do not mean tyres!

Walking from room to room, you could be forgiven for

Gretton, owner of the Bass, Ratcliffe and Gretton brewery. Lord Gretton is said to have been far more interested in the fashionable hunting circles nearby than Stapleford's own extensive facilities and in accordance with his social aspirations, he undertook radical building work on the house. Several reception rooms and guest rooms were added, and when everything was finished, Stapleford Park reflected the beauty and grandeur of English architecture through the ages, allowing Lord Gretton to entertain in true Edwardian style.

A century on and little has changed: the estate retains its regal charm, though maybe the atmosphere is a little more relaxed than it was a hundred years ago.

It was this mixture of old and new that attracted Peter de Savary to Stapleford in 1996, when he bought it and created the English rural 'outpost' of his selective Carnegie Club.

The recent multi-million pound expenditure has created something unique, luxurious and welcoming for the enjoyment of house guests at Stapleford.

Wandering around the house and gardens is an unforgettable

mistaking this for a royal household.

The Grand Hall and Saloon being especially impressive, contrast nicely with the more intimate Drawing Room, Morning Room and Library.

The main dining room is the Grinling Gibbons Room, where the walls are adorned with wood carvings by the eponymous artist.

One can roam all day, constantly finding new works of art and hidden rooms in this labyrinth of style.

The estate is 500 acres and the gardens have been lovingly renovated over the past seven years.

Behind the walled garden stands the church of St. Mary Magdalen.

Built in 1783 by the Earl of Harborough, the church is outstanding in the Gothic field for its date, with all its original features.

As well as riding, which is based at the Victorian stables, you can practice falconry and archery, play tennis, croquet and now a few holes of golf at the new Carnegie Links Golf Academy.

And as if this were not enough, let us not forget the Carnegie Clarins Spa, a stunning beauty and health centre in the Orangery with a mosaic-tiled indoor pool.

The complex houses the pool, a solarium, sauna, steam room, gym and massage parlour and is ideally equipped to relieve any excess tension.

The First Baron John Gretton created his dream - a place of leisure on the grandest scale; now it is once again possible to live that dream.

21

BLAKES

You find them on film sets and in immaculate design offices. They live in villas and manor houses with huge walled gardens.

They shop in the chic boutiques of Paris and dine in exclusive restaurants in New York.

Hair blowing in the wind, they drive their convertibles on the Croisette in Cannes, go hunting on the vast hunting grounds of Scotland and sip champagne at international polo matches.

They crowd the ski slopes of St. Moritz and Gstaad and sunbathe on the Costa Smeralda.

Their life is one big challenge, one endless quest for new experiences, new surprises. This is the fascinating, glittering word of success.

But they are the exception, for they are the 'jet-set of creativity', the 'jet-set of good taste'.

They think that for them, the world holds no secrets. Until their limousine turns into Roland Gardens in South Kensington, and stops in front of a dark green 19th-century Victorian façade which is in sharp contrast to the other red-brick houses.

This is not an hotel, it's a museum; this is not London, it's the world with a London accent.

Fifty different rooms, fifty different experiences and surpri-

110

ses, fifty dreams.

"There's only one Blakes", says Anouska Hempel about her temple of residence. It is hard to imagine, but just as you can admire the Crown Jewels in the Tower, stone by stone, so every corner and detail at Blakes can be admired.

My visit to Blakes becomes a journey through strange continents and different times. In the reception area, next to my suitcase, stand trunks from colonial times.

It is as if a Maharajah has just arrived, or at least his luggage. The room is filled with cane furniture and even an

enormous white parasol, and against the wall a magnificent birdcage with a whistling parakeet.

Beneath the parasol, a staircase leads down to a peaceful room of culinary and visual delights.

Directly opposite me is the restaurant, where world-class international cuisine with strong eastern influences is served.

Here, too, Anouska Hempel has left her personal stamp. The same goes for the decoration: on the walls hang national costumes and jewelry of Thai and Eastern moun-

113

tain peoples. Behind me is the softly-lit bar, and to the right is the Chinese Room, with wonderful wall paintings and unusual small tables around a larger table laden with books on art and design.

Evening falls over the courtyard. Once, this must have been a simple backyard, but now, it has a magic mediterranean atmosphere -once again, the work of Anouska Hempel.

The exotic atmosphere continues: from the courtyard, a door leads to the Honeymoon Suite, the "White Room".

It is like being on safari here: a four-poster bed with transparent curtains resembling a mosquito net.

The room itself, in virginal white, seems to come straight out of a residence on the Avenue Foch in Paris. The atmosphere is wonderful!

We go upstairs and open another door: this room looks like a Bedouin tent in the Sahara, with white-painted earthenware pots beside the bed, and unusual white and beige linen items of clothing hanging on the wall...

We pass rooms full of antique furniture and beds in the style of Napoleon

III and arrive back in England: the Library Room.

It looks like a huge library with hundreds of old books.

Until we want to take one and leaf through it. They turn out to be a trompe l'oeil, but one of superior artistry.

And then there is the highlight of the hotel: Room 109 (The One O Nine), otherwise known as the Cardinal Suite.

It is out of this world, with a magnificent four-poster bed, with gold, red, burgundy and blue everywhere, and walls painted in faux tortoiseshell. Hidden lighting and a wealth of heavy curtains remind one of Shakespeare's time.

"There is only one Blakes", we would wholeheartedly agree.

But one last thing: the hotel is renowned for a service which is of no use to me, and no doubt to most of us: the way it protects and shields the privacy of its guests from the press, the fans, and the public in general.

It seems that Robert de Niro, Jack Nicholson, Mick Jagger, Lacroix, Jean Paul Gaultier and many others do appreciate it.

115

22

BAILIFFSCOURT

116   Although Bailiffscourt in the middle of a flat landscape near the murmuring sea, contains many secrets of centuries past, its best guarded secret must be its final destiny.

For it was not until 1927 that a real fairytale came true here. Lord Moyne, who was then still known as Walter Guiness, descendant of the world famous brewers' family and a member of the British Parliament, and his wife Evelyn, daughter of the fourteenth Baron of Buchan, lived at Grosvenor Place in London, in a manor house that reflected Lady Evelyn's passion for the Middle Ages.

She found a soul mate in Amyas Phillips, an antiques dealer whom she had happened to meet on one of her searches for medieval beauty.

But the delights of the countryside beckoned.

In the Twenties, London high society gradually got into the habit of going on outings in the automobile, spending a few days in the country or at the seaside.

Thus one day, Lord and Lady Moyne ended up in Climping, where they spent weekends in a neglected but romantic old building which was known in the area as 'the hut'.

make it into a truly extraordinary country retreat which would exude an atmosphere of times long past.

Perhaps it was because of the traumatic events of World War I, but during the decade following it people began to realise how relative their fixed values really were.

They went back to an idyllic notion of nature and, where building was concerned, to the long gone Tudor style.

The architects tried to use and retrieve as many authentic materials as possible.

Inspired by Lady Moyne, Mr. Phillips had the farm house pulled down and the original stone window and door frames from the twelfth and thirteenth centuries restored.

These were then integrated into the wonderful manor house that was erected in golden yellow old Somerset sandstone.

In order to build the property, age-old doors and beams were sought for and found and whole buildings were moved.

The fifteenth-century gatehouse came from Loxwood and was rebuilt next to a seventeenth-century house with half-timber façade from Old Basing in Hampshire.

On the north side, he had a separate building erected, the 'Guest House' which Lady Moyne used as her private residence and which was connected by a tunnel to the main building, where her husband continued to live with the children.

This made a romantic courtyard where, in fair weather, it is a pleasure to dine outside.

When word reached them that a notable from the area wanted to parcel out their idyllic country retreat, Lord Moyne bought the estate, which comprised seven hundred and fifty acres, including a farm and a Norman chapel.

This thirteenth century chapel had once been given to the Seez abbey in Normandy, after the Norman conquest, and the abbot of Seez sent a monk down as a bailiff.

Hence the name 'Bailiffscourt'.

Lord and Lady Moyne had great plans for Bailiffscourt, and they asked their good friend, antiques dealer Phillips, to

The aforementioned Norman chapel where it all started centuries ago, was beautifully restored, as an ode to the past, and is now used as service quarters.

In 1933, when the buildings were finished, Phillips started to concentrate on the garden.

Hundreds of trees, some more than 25 years old, were uprooted from the woods on the Downs and, with varying success, replanted in Bailiffscourt's meagre soil, which had been eroded by sea, salt and sand.

In the following years, the Moynes's guests, such as English writers, dukes and duchesses, enjoyed their hospitality during romantic picnics and wonderful parties on the estate.

However, tragedy hits even high society. The fairytale came to a dramatic end when Lady Moyne died in 1939, six years after her life's dream had been completed.

A few months later, when World War II broke out, the family left Bailiffscourt for good, never to return.

In November 1944 Lord Moyne, who was Minister for the Middle East at the time, was killed in Egypt by the Stern band.

Luckily, the spirit of hospitality and refinement still lives on in the work of Sandy and Anne Goodman, who receive their hotel guests in a way that could only be emulated by Lady Moyne herself.

23

ARMATHWAITE HALL

"Speaking of romance, is there anything more romantic than Armathwaite Hall with its lovely habit of drawing Bassenthwaite in a sheet of silver and orange to its very doors?
With the trees to guard it, and the history that inhabits it, and the lake that stretches before it, it is a house of perfect and irresistible atmosphere".
Armathwaite Hall has always been as beautiful, but not always as peaceful and quiet as Sir Walpole describes it here.
The Fletcher-Vane family, who owned the idyllic estate for four

generations, defended it against anyone who dared to threaten them.
There is still a story about the 'Battle of Bassenthwaite' which is supposed to have taken place between 1830 and 1940.
For many years, the Fletcher-Vanes had been at variance with the Count of Egremont, who owned the whole lake, apart from three fishing grounds which belonged to Armathwaite Hall. During one of their disagreements, the count decided to build a pier on the lake.
The Vanes did not like this at all, and when the count's builders turned up in the morning, the Vanes came running hell-for-leather with their servants.
The story goes that many of them, in their hurry not to miss the fight, had not even taken the time to put on their boots, and came onto the battlefield in stockinged feet.
That much 'enthusiasm' put the count's people off and they ran away or jumped in the lake.

In 1850, the Hall came into the hands of Mr Boustead, whose family had interests in tea plantations in Ceylon, and in 1880 it was bought by Thomas Hartley, a local mine owner and member of Parliament.

He converted Armathwaite Hall to the rural Victorian manor house it is today.

After Mr Hartley's death, the estate was put up for sale with these words: "The Hall, private fishing grounds for salmon and trout, six farmhouses, The Castle Inn, many cottages and 268 acres of land. " Everything was sold, apart from Armathwaite Hall itself and the surrounding parklands adjoining the lake.

Luckily ,the owner of the Keswick hotel bought the manor house, and six months later, in 1930, Armathwaite Hall, completely renovated, started a new life as an hotel.

The present owners, the Graves family, bought the hotel in 1976 with the intention of making it into an establishment of superior quality, from which a number of activities could be organised. In 1989 they bought Coalbeck Farm, an adjoining farmhouse, which now houses an equestrial centre and an animal farm park.

The Graves' dynamic enthusiasm adds another dimension to a stay here. An incredible number of activities are organised: safaris by quad bikes and four-wheel drive vehicles, mountain biking, archery, guided walks through the Lake District, mountain climbing, balloon rides, golf, croquet, fishing and watercolour painting lessons, with the most beautiful spots in the Lake District as subjects.

And as Sir Walpole wrote his impressions of Armathwaite Hall, so the great poet of the area, Wordsworth, wrote about the Lake District: "no other area in the country offers such a variety of sublime beauty on such a small surface, suffused with a whirling play of shadow and light."

Mountains such as 'The Old Man' rise suddenly from the

surface of still little lakes. And rivers find their way through the idyllic green land-scape past villages and towns in all colours imaginable: Keswick, Windermere, Grasmere and Ambleside.

This is England at its most beautiful and the best way to discover it is by following

the 48 kilometres long 'Poets' Trail'. When you get back to the hotel, the fine cui-sine of master chef Kevin Dowling awaits you, with its French and English inspired Cumbrian specialities.

You may have a drink in the bar and maybe go to your 'Up the Tower' suite, your own 'tower' in the manor house, with a sunken bath and an area where you can have your private candlelit dinner, enjoying an impressive view of the Lake District and Bassenthwaite Lake.

The only thing you'll have to imagine is the pier, for it never materialised...

HARTWELL HOUSE

It was very quiet in the Library at Hartwell House.

The representatives of the French Republic, the French Royal family and the royal household watched with bated breath while Louis XVIII signed his accession to the throne, making France a monarchy again – albeit it only for a short time – after the restless years of the Revolution and the Napoleonic era.

Thirteen years before, he had fled Paris like a thief in the night, using an English name.

For years, he had wandered through Europe, pursued by the French revolutionary armies, until 1809, when England, which was at war with Napoleon, gave him permission to take up residence at the magnificent Hartwell House.

This is where he lived with the exiled French Royal Court, some 140 in all.

It was a mixed company: members of the royal family, such as the daughter of Louis XVI, the Duchess of Angoulème, the Duke de Gramont and the Archbishop of Reims, all with their servants and members of their retinue.

Now, Louis XVIII exchanged Hartwell House for the Tuileries and the palace of St. Cloud in Paris.

Hartwell House has always played an important role in history, even a thousand years ago.

In the Domesday Book, it was mentioned as the property of William Peverel, son of William the Conqueror, and John, Count of Montaigne, who would succeed his brother, Richard Lionheart, as King of England in 1199. For generations, the Lee family, ancestors of General Robert E. Lee who led the Confederate armies during the American Civil war, left their mark on Hartwell House.

The current house dates from the beginning of the 17th century and it has both Jacobean and Georgian façades. At the entrance, there is a statue of Frederick, Prince of Wales, on horseback.

You enter the Great Hall, an imposing room in English baroque style. Beyond it lies the oak-clad bar with copies of original paintings of the gardens by the Spanish artist Nebot.

Opulent rooms like The Morning Room, The Drawing Room and The Library, which look out on the gardens, were built in the Georgian era around 1760.

The spectacular main staircase is partly Jacobean and decorated with extraordinary carved wooden figures.

Hartwell has 31 rooms and suites in the main building, spread over three floors.

The rooms on the first floor have all been named after members of the Bourbon dynasty and other prominent figures who once stayed here.

On the roof there is a terrace where the French exiles grew vegetables and raised rabbits and chickens.

Now, it is a wonderful place for guests to relax and sunbathe. In the Sloane Dining Room, designed in the style of the eminent architect Sir John Soane, a creative cuisine, recently rewarded three AA rosettes, is served.

In the 18th-century stables near the park, another 16 luxurious rooms and suites can be found.

And speaking of the park, this is a wonderful attraction in itself.

It was landscaped in the style of Capability Brown and is adorned with monuments and 18th-century pavilions.

It also contains the remains of a church, a croquet lawn, tennis courts and a large pond full of trout, where

guests can fish to their heart's content. The Hartwell Spa is housed in a beautiful building, designed as an orangery, also inspired by Sir Soane.
And the Spa Buttery, in a gallery with a view of the indoor pool; serves

drinks and light meals. The vale of Aylesbury is one of the most picturesque areas in the county of Buckinghamshire. It has wonderful manor houses, such as Blenheim Palace, Claydon House, Waddesdon

Manor, and Woburn Abbey.
Louis XVIII was a hedonist: rather than bothering with politics, he liked to walk in the wonderful park, went shopping incognito for vegetables and flowers in the market at nearby

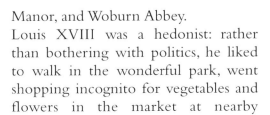

Aylesbury and made trips to Oxford, Cambridge and Bath.
In short, he found pleasure in everything and we can only advise you to do the same during your stay at Hartwell House.

25

THE GREENWAY

The Greenway is a perfect example of a real English 'country house hotel'.

David and Valerie White, the current owners, have made a very special place out of this Elizabethan house, steeped in history.

And that history is all to do with one fascinating person: William Lawrence.

William was born in 1636 and grew up in London.

But he much preferred to stay on the beautiful property his uncle had built half a century before at Shurdington, later to be named The

Greenway Estate and which his old uncle had left to him in his will.

Together with his brother, Isaac, he made plans to maintain the honour of the family who had been owners of Shurdington Estate for generations, and to restore the family seat to its former glory. Isaac, however, signed on with the East India Company and left for India to make his fortune.

William married Anne and managed the estate.

But after the birth of their son, William junior, whom he worshipped, fate dealt him a cruel blow.

Isaac died of dysentry caught in India, leaving nothing, and a few years later, within two months of each other, William's wife and son died.

He was a broken man who wrote these words to Anne's best friend: 'Anne's death has taken away a life that was very dear to me, but with William's death, I have lost my future and my progeny.'

From then on, the memory of his loved ones and his ancestors ruled his life, and he made a strange, but fascinating decision: he would dedicate the rest of his life to designing a

wonderful garden around his manor house, in their memory.

It would be a Dutch–French inspired garden, full of symbolism about life and mortality. For example, a small, simple front garden symbolised 'childhood'.

A second front garden, larger and more beautiful, represented 'youth'.

A large green lawn, which could be reached through a corridor of pillars, meant 'adulthood and lust for life' and an ancient orchard represented 'old age'.

131

A second meadow with dwarf trees referred to 'new life to come'.

Today, the shapes that William Lawrence used so symbolically, are still clearly visible, and some of the 300-year-old trees still stand witness to his love for his family.

In the 18th century, the name of the estate was changed to 'The Greenway', for next to the hotel a path of that name, which dates from Roman times, leads to a prehistoric burial ground

'Green Way' means a 'drove' road or path and refers to the fact that this must have been a safe passage for livestock, protecting them from wild animals living on the wooded hills.

Owners of The Greenway came and went and finally, in 1947, it opened as a country house hotel with a service close to perfection.

Today the reception rooms full of antiques, fresh flowers and open fireplaces all give access to the gardens.

The nineteen luxury bedrooms, a number of which are to be found in the restored coach house, have been tastefully furnished and provide every creature comfort.

The view over the landscaped grounds, with the Cotswold Hills behind it, is absolutely stunning. The restaurant looks out onto the sunken garden and the romantic lily pond and offers gourmet food, accompanied by excellent wines.

The Greenway stands on the edge of the Regency spa town of Cheltenham, at the foot of the Cotswolds, a hilly green landscape full of pretty little towns and villages such as Broadway, Chipping Campden, Bourton-on-the-Water and Bibury.

Life dealt William Lawrence some cruel blows, but he managed to build a permanent memento of his family and to turn his sadness into the creation of a unique estate, the beauty of which the hotel guests of The Greenway can thoroughly enjoy.

26

THE LONDON OUTPOST
OF THE CARNEGIE CLUB

Behind this adventurous name is a fascinating story, the fantastic tale of Andrew Carnegie, a poor weaver's son, who became one of the richest people in the world.

He was born in Scotland in 1835. When weaving mills became more and more productive thanks to the steam engine, the family -like many hundreds of thousands at the time- had to emigrate to the New World, with no means of livelihood. To help provide for the family, thirteen-year old Andrew started work helping out in an American weaving mill. He was so industrious that he was soon offered a job as an errand-boy, and later as a telegraph operator.

Soon, he was noticed by Thomas A. Scott, head of the Pennsylvania Railroad, who gave him a job with the railway and advised him to buy some shares in the Adams Express Company. It was his first business venture and it was a success.

From then on, everything Andrew Carnegie touched, turned to gold.

At thirty, he had interests in the steel industry and owned steamers on the Great Lakes, railway companies and oil-wells.

He became the 'Steel King' of America, but in his heart he remained a Scotsman.

That is why he bought a castle in the country of his birth: Scibo Castle.

From there, he reigned over his world empire, and this is where he received his guests: King Edward VII, the Rockefellers - the list was endless.

But success and wealth are volatile, and several years ago, Scibo lay deserted, with weeds growing in the gardens and on the façades.

Until Peter de Savary restored the castle and founded 'The Carnegie Club', where members could enjoy the legendary atmosphere of hospitality and exclusivity so typical of Carnegie.

As a service to the members of this exclusive club, a typical London town house was bought as a 'pied à terre' in the capital.

It was a Victorian private residence in Cadogan Gardens, an exclusive street not far from Sloane Square.

Once, the London Outpost was a private home. Now, it has been restored magnificently and comfortably for the benefit of its guests. Each of the eleven air-conditioned rooms has its own personal style.

The 'Club' atmosphere can mainly be felt in the reception rooms: the snooker room, the library and the conservatory, where breakfast and light meals are served.

The quiet, picturesque Cadogan Gardens area is the perfect place for a special stay in London.

Harrods and the Knightsbridge museums are within walking distance and the lively King's Road is no more than a hundred metres away.

The City and The West End can easily be reached by taxi or underground from Sloane Square.

Some of the best restaurants in town are within walking distance of The London Outpost. And it is like the hotel itself says: "Let us take your luggage to your room. Let us turn back your sheets and fluff up your pillows.

Let us shine your shoes and bring you your newspaper. Let us drive you around London to Harrods, to the parks, to the Tower, Parliament or a musical.

We are always at your disposal, for at 'The London Outpost', you have found your home in London."

Discreet and exclusive, just as Carnegie himself would have wanted it.

27

ETTINGTON PARK

Nestling on the banks of the River Stour some five miles from Stratford upon Avon, the home of William Shakespeare, stands Ettington Park, a gem of a house which, surrounded by terrace-shaped gardens and green lawns, evokes the atmosphere of a Victorian folly. For some nine hundred years, the estate has been the ancestral home of the Shirley family, one of the most respected families in the county of Warwickshire.

Unique in England, they can claim the oldest direct lineage in the country, having appeared in the Domesday Book in 1085, during the reign of William the Conqueror.

Walking around the estate one can imagine the days when Shakespeare visited the family for tea, whilst the three hundred year-old fir trees and remains of a twelfth-century church recall the days when the village of Ettington bordered the house.

The existing mansion is striking as you approach it down a long line of lime trees.

Built in the highly fashionable neo-gothic style of the late 18th century, it could be described as an eccentric combination of an 18th-century French chateau and an ecclesiastical edifice.

Four different kinds of locally quarried stone were used, although the lush honey tones

of the Cotswold limestone, which seem to glow in the late evening sun, prevail.

Designed by a contemporary of Charles Barry, who designed the Houses of Parliament in London, the architectural details and craftsmanship have been recognised, as the house is listed Grade 1 by English Heritage.

As you walk around the exterior, you will no doubt admire the sheer quality of the building and think of the hours of work the local skilled artisans must have taken during its five-year construction. All for the cost of £ 15,000!

Over 14 external stone etchings can be seen, each representing interesting features of the

family history through the centuries. For example, one relief represents the imprisonment of a member of the Shirley family by Oliver Cromwell in 1656.

You enter the house via the palm-filled cloistered conservatory with its beautiful Victorian tiles.

It feels as if time has stood still as you are welcomed into the impressive hall, with its massive Elizabethan oak mantelpiece exuding the warmth and smell of the burning oak fire. All around you, you feel of the dignity of this ancestral home, with its elaborate plasterwork, marble pillars and truly magnificent reception rooms.

Emblazoned throughout the house is the motto 'Loyal je Suis' which originated from the days when a member of the family married the daughter of the Earl of Essex.

The former ballroom is now the Great Drawing Room. One can imagine the elegant balls that must have been held under the gilt ceiling designed by Italian crafstmen...The dining room is oak-panelled and adorned with over 70 of the family's crests.

As you walk through the 40-acre park with its ancient cedar trees, fountains and numerous underground passages, you are aware of a sense of tranquility and peacefulness, shrouded by the history of a bygone era.

Now fully restored, most of the 48 bedrooms offer stunning views across the park and rolling hills. Each room has been individually decorated, using the finest fabrics, with numerous

objets d'art and antiques.

The Kingmaker Chamber has been decorated in medieval style with the support and advice of Warwick Castle. It boasts a crimson canopied bedroom and gallery overlooking the flagstone sitting room, whilst the bathroom has a bath the size of a swimming pool.

Other rooms include '10 and 11 Downing Street', with a strong parliamentarian theme, which have been created to bear witness to the family's association with the House of Commons, whilst the four-poster Stour and Shirley suites offer similarly impressive accommodation.

All in all, Ettington Park still recalls the days of a grand private house complete with the family pets, dogs and a flock of peacocks.

28

THE ROMAN CAMP

In the walled garden, the gardener was trimming the rose bushes.

He was an elderly gentleman, wearing a straw hat and a green apron, obviously enjoying his work on this wonderful morning. Beyond the walls of the Italian-style flower garden, adorned with beautiful statues, a lawn sloped down on one side towards a murmuring river, and a pink-painted romantic lodge could be seen on the other side. It was a dainty-looking, lovely house with turrets, in a style reminiscent of a French chateau.

Suddenly, a black coach, drawn by two horses, came up the drive and stopped in front of the house.

Two distinguished-looking gentlemen in high hats descended and were welcomed by the groom.

He pointed in the direction of the garden and, carrying a white document, the gentlemen proceeded over the lawn towards the gardener.

Reverently, they bowed in greeting and handed him the envelope, which carried the royal seal of Buckingham Palace.

The 'gardener' was no less than Viscount Esher, confi-

dant of King George V and owner of the idyllic estate. Accompanied by the king's two representatives, he entered the house and closed the door behind him.

Lord Esher was a prominent figure in Great Britain around the turn of the century.

Not only was he on intimate terms with kings and Prime Ministers; he was also Chairman of the Committee of Defence of the Commonwealth and

Governor of Windsor Castle. He was married to the daughter of the Belgian Minister at the Court of St. James, and father to Dorothy Brett, a friend of Virginia Woolf's and an artist who moved in the highest literary circles.

And in spite of his busy social and political life, Lord Esher still found time to retreat to his beloved estate, The Roman Camp. The name refers to a nearby Roman fort, which in the first century was part of the Roman defence line against attacks of the Highlanders. On one side, the river formed a natural defence, and on the other three sides of the settlement, high earth fortifications were built.

In the 17th century, The Roman Camp was a modest hunting lodge on the estate of the Barons of Moray, one of Scotland's oldest and most prominent families; in the Middle Ages, one of their ancestors married Christian, sister of Robert the Bruce.

Another Baron Mornay was Regent of Scotland during the childhood years of King James I, son of Mary Queen of Scots.

In 1897 The Roman Camp started its 'third' life when Lord Esher bought the estate.

With great enthusiasm, he had the gardens landscaped and the old lodge redecorated in a truly splendid way.

He had the library built on, as well as the lounge and the guest rooms. Several turrets - one of them housing a minuscule chapel- made the fairy-tale complete.

As early as 1939, The Roman Camp became an hotel, now managed by Eric and Marion Brown.

The small, romantic hotel with an open fire nearly always burning in the reception area and in the restaurant, is surrounded by twenty acres of land, and is situated just behind the main street of the town of Callander.

An ideal spot for tourists, for this is the crossroads of Scotland.

To the south lie the Lowlands, to the north the Highlands – this is the region where another illustrious inhabitant, freedom fighter Rob Roy Mc Gregor, operated. The 18th-century hero of the people was a freebooter and cattle thief, who stole back what the Duke of Montrose took from him when he confiscated his land and possessions.

The Roman Camp lies at the foot of the Trossachs, an incredibly beautiful, idyllic area with high hills and wonderful lochs.

When you visit, do take a boat ride on Loch Katrine in the old steamboat SS Sir Walter Scott, named after the famous Scottish author who described the life of Rob Roy in one of his books. You would be hard put to find another place in Scotland that has so much variety and so many attractions to offer: Stirling Castle, Callender House, Edinburgh and Glasglow are close by.

But most of all, simply enjoy this wonderful hotel.

When evening falls, sit by the open fire in Lord Esher's reading room, take Sir Walter Scott's book and, sipping a glass of Scottish whiskey, dream about the adventurous world of Rob Roy Mc Gregor.

145

29

KINNAIRD

The evening sun threw a red glow over the barren hills of the plateau and the contrast with the deep blue, still waters of Loch Skiach became greater all the time.

The three friends rowed to the bank and pulled their little boat onto land. It had been a memorable day and the catch, some twenty pike, were stored in a cool-box in the Land Rover.

Every year, the three of them went off for a few days to talk about childhood memories and the practice of their favourite sport, fishing, preferably in an idyllic environment. They had heard many stories about Kinnaird, but the beauty and grandeur of the 9,000 acre estate exceeded their greatest expectations.

Imagine: far below in the green valley stood a stunning manor house in the middle of a park, with views of the river Tay, which for three miles runs through this large estate.

One sees green hills with farm houses and cottages, and as one climbs higher, the breath-taking splendour of a rough, deserted landscape is revealed, providing views of the far hills, and one is surrounded by flocks of sheep and hundreds of pheasants.

There are also woodlands where foxes and deer hide, and three lochs for fishing.

Darkness fell quickly now.

The first call of an owl came from the woods and the silhouettes of the Highlands, way up north, became vague. With difficulty, the Land Rover crept down over the uneven terrain, toward a different world.

The house and gardens were lit as in a fairy tale when the friends entered the drive.

On the lawn, the other hotel guests sat in a circle around a group of musicians.

Still in their fishing clothes; the three men found a place amongst the beautifully-dressed audience, for the music was not to be

147

missed.

An hour later, after a good shower, our friends, now indistinguishable from the rest of the company, had supper in the restaurant with its beautifully painted panelling. They savoured the fine cuisine of the Chef, who showed himself worthy of the many awards he had received.

The delicious food and excellent wine fortified them for a game of billiards after dinner.

The friends moved to the cosy Billiard Room where the open fire cast an inviting glow. But more than the game, it was the giant salmon that caught their interest.

The fish were displayed in glass cases and all of them, some more than one metre long and weighing up to 50 pounds, had been caught on the Kinnaird Beat back in the 1920s, by members of the Ward family, the owners of Kinnaird.

While our friends were commenting on the trophies, Mrs Constance Ward, the present owner and proprietor, entered the room.

With amusement she told them that on October 11th 1928, her father-in-law, The Hon. Sir John Ward, was fishing at Kinnaird and caught a salmon weighing no less than 44 lbs, but when he proudly arrived at the house with his heavy catch, his cousin, Lady Lettice Ward, stood there waiting for him with a fish weighing 50 pounds!

This estate record has never been broken.

And this brings us to the history of the Kinnaird Estate. The original part of Kinnaird House was built in the 1770s. More was added by the succeeding owners

in the 1860s who, it is interesting to note, employed the young (at that time) Thomas Carlyle as a tutor to their two sons. Later, the Kinnaird Estate became part of the enormous land-holdings of the neighbour-ing Duke of Atholl, during which period the house become a dower house for the senoir duchesses.

In 1927 the Kinnaird holding was purchased by The Hon. Lady Ward, daughter-in-law of the second Earl of Dudley. Her son, Reginald, mar-ried an American, Constance Cluett, and after the death of her hus-band in 1987, Mrs Ward decided to open the house as an hotel.

It is no surprise that Mrs Ward has made the house into something exquisite, for her family owned two distinguished period Inns in the United States.

The eight rooms and the suite at Kinnaird are named after farms and

other places on the estate and each has been decorated differently and tastefully with family antiques, beautiful fabrics and gas-log open fires which welcome the visitor.

The hotel is filled with beautifully arranged bouquets of fresh flowers, furniture of superior quality, Chinese porcelain and family souvenirs. The main reception room is panelled in cedar wood and this is where one can play a quiet game of backgammon whilst sipping a single malt whisky by the open fire.

If one is not keen on fishing there is a choice of croquet, tennis, pheasant shooting during the season, drives around the estate and hills, and

the possibility of long walks to the Lochs of Kinnaird which will make your stay unforgettable.

Here, in the Grampian mountains, beats the heart of Scotland. Close by the hotel is the little town of Dunkeld with its picturesque square and the lovely church itself, sitting by the river and surrounded by greenery.

The drive to Blair Castle is as beautiful as the castle itself, and last but not least, there is Pitlochry with its famous 'salmon ladder', where the salmon that the fishermen did not manage to catch lower down the river face a new obstacle here –which they conquer seemingly without difficulty.

From the underwater observation station, a visitor can see thousands of salmon leap over the great differences in level at this point in the river.

All in all – Scotland at its best!

30

BALBIRNIE HOUSE

It was on a day sometime in the year 1843 that he was found, lifeless, in his chair in his house in Sweetbank. Neil Ballingal had reached the age of 93, and had devoted 73 years of his life to the management of Balbirnie and the Balfour family. He was the only man in history who saw the estate develop from an unremarkable house in a bare landscape to a monumental and breath-takingly beautiful sand-coloured Georgian manor house, surrounded by one of the most wonderful parks in the Kingdom of Fife.

The Balfours were very fortunate that they had clerks like the Ballingals. From 1770 to 1916, sons following their fathers, they carefully and dutifully managed the estate. Historians, too, should be grateful to the Ballingals, for their account books and minutes paint an accurate picture of the evolution through the centuries of estates such as this one.

So let's have a look at their archives. These date back to the year 1312, when John de Balbrennie, follower of Robert the Bruce, and responsible for the defence of Dundee against possible attacks by King Edward of England, gave his name to the estate. Over the years, 'Balbrennie' changed to 'Balbirnie'. Later in the Middle Ages, during the next 350 years, the estate had many owners. In 1642 an old Scottish family, the Balfours, acquired Balbirnie.

For a century, the Balfours lived in the manor house protected on all sides from the cold northern wind by the sloping of the landscape. Unlike many other gentlemen who lived on this kind of estate, in 1777 John Balfour decided not to pull down the existing house in order to build a more modern one, but to greatly extend the house with new rooms. For 90 years, John, and later his son, General Robert Balfour, financed the transformation and extension work out of their profits from coal mining and agriculture.

This resulted in one of the most impressive Georgian-style manor houses in Scotland, with a main entrance resembling a Greek temple. In 1779, virtually at the same time as the start of the building work, landscape architect Robert Robinson sketched some innovative proposals for the landscaping of the park, in the style of Capability Brown. In the annals of 1794, the park was described as: 'a wonderfully romantic place with rolling lawns bordered by plants'.

On a hill near the manor house, stables were built, surrounding a courtyard. Nowadays, the Balbirnie Centre of Arts and Crafts is housed here. The Balfours used to live in London from January to June, and then spend the summer and autumn at Balbirnie, where they received family and friends on their way to the north or returning south. Some 12 to 14 people could regularly be found dining in the sumptious dining room.

Now, Balbirnie House is a luxury hotel, owned and personally managed by the Russell family who have many years of experience in the hotel business. In 1996, Balbirnie House was chosen as 'Hotel of the year' in Scotland.

The 18-hole Balbirnie Park Golf Course is beautifully integrated into the park, which boasts one of the most beautiful rhododendron plantations in Eastern Scotland. Each hole has its own name, which has an historical significance.

For instance, the 8th hole is called 'Target Park', for this is where archery was once practiced.

The luxurious hotel maintains the intimacy and cosiness of the old days – this can still be felt in the cocktail bar named 'The Old Library', in the restaurant with its view of the park, the beautifully decorated rooms and the lounge with its unique oblong shape.

Great points of historical and tourist attraction in Scotland form a circle around Balbirnie House.

In all four directions, the best of what Scotland has to offer can be found: in the east, the idyllic village of Falkland with its castle, the tiny harbours of East Neuk and the golfers' paradise of St. Andrews; in the south, Edinburgh and the manor houses of Hopetoun and Linlithgow; in the west, the impressive Loch Lomond and the Trossachs, the most romantic area in Scotland; and finally, in the north, the historic castles of Scone Palace, Glarnis Castle and Blair Castle, and the salmon ladders of Pitlochry.

'Balbirnie House',
one of the most impressive Georgian
manor houses in Scotland,
has a façade like a Greek temple.

155

31

ARDANAISEIG HOTEL

It was a wonderful Sunday morning. The sun was pleasantly warm and chased the chill from the deep waters of Loch Awe.

When the fog lifted, the sound of oars could be heard, and the cheerful laughter and singing of clear girls' voices. In the mist, hazy silhouettes formed, which, when they came nearer, turned out to be small boats.

The leading one was the largest, and two girls handled the oars while an older gentleman in a white suit and straw hat watched contentedly.

They were members of the Campbell family who -weather

permitting- rowed to the other side of the loch to attend High Mass. Every Sunday, Colonel James Archibald Campbell asked two of his many daughters to row him to Cladich and back, while the rest of the family and the servants followed in other boats.

Archibald had every reason to be happy: he had a wonderful family, no money worries and from his boat he could see his romantic manor house, situated on the very tip of the isthmus on the shores of Loch Awe.

Nature was of an almost unreal beauty here: the loch was dotted with green islands, with ruins of former convents and the graves of the Dukes of Argyll, and high above the hills surrounding the clear Loch stood the mighty mountain of Ben Cruachan.

The boats set course to a small island in the loch, several hundred yards from the manor house.

Two servants were busily spreading blankets on the green grass.

They took fresh rolls and champagne from big hampers: the company was expected for a picnic on their private island 'Eilean a Chomlraidh'.

The god-fearing colonel died in 1879, and one year later, the estate, which had been called New Inverawe up till then, was sold to Sir John Ainsworth, who had interests in the iron and coal industry.

Long before, it had been decided within the Campbell family that, if the family estate ever had to be sold, it could no longer be called New Inverawe.

Sir John therefore changed the name to 'Ardanaiseig', which means 'point of land near the ferry'. Small boats once used to carry people from here to the other side of the Loch.

After Sir John's death in 1932, Ardanaiseig became the property of his son, Sir Thomas.

He was passionate about plants and flowers and spent a lot of time cultivating the garden and park.

Unfortunately, during World War II, the estate was badly neglected. And after the war, Sir Thomas moved to Ireland.

The next owners, the McCallums, restored the 100 acre park to its former glory and had thousands of exotic plants and trees imported from distant continents, as far as the foothills of the Himalayas, which have a similar climate.

The gardens are now famous.

The Baronial-style manor house as we know it now, was commissioned by Archibald Campbell in 1834.

The architect was no less than William Burn who also designed Bowhill castle for the Duke of Buccleuch, as well as a great number of important 19th century buildings in Edinburgh.

Since then, Ardanaiseig has become an idyllic luxury hotel, reflecting its charm and romance.

There are open fireplaces, a restaurant where soft candlelight reflects in the silverware and crystal glasses, a cosy bar, an exquisite 19th century lounge, with many of the bedrooms having a view of the loch and gardens.

Ardanaiseig's owner , professor Bennie Gray, antiquarian and naturalist, wants to go beyond the boundaries of hotelkeeping: Ardanaiseig strives to bring as many 18th century Scottish works of art and antiques as possible back to the Highlands, and to give them a home in the manor house.

In the hotel, guests can admire the collections that Mr Gray has found.

156

158

Other treats give an extra dimension to a stay here: guests are met by boat at the station of Loch Awe and brought to the hotel, sea planes can land on the Loch, so that guests, after enjoying a fascinating flight over Lochs, Highlands, creeks and

islands, can be met by the hotel boat. A picnic on the private island 'Eilean a Chomlraidh' makes the dream complete even though you might not be rowed there by two of Sir Archibald's daughters.

159

32

LLANGOED HALL

One cart after the other, laden with precious furniture and household goods, creaked down the lane from Llangoed Hall.

A coach stopped in front of the porch of the beautiful manor house and a man painfully descended. With tears in his eyes, Mister Williams threw a last glance at the elegant façade and the beautiful park that lay between the woods and the river Wye. Slowly, he climbed back into the coach, never to return.

The unfortunate man had simply gambled away Llangoed Hall, which had been the home of his

family for centuries...

This tragedy took place in 1880, but the story starts in 560 A.D., when on the banks of this river a house must have stood, the legendary 'White Palace'.

The story goes that the first Parliament of Wales sat here. In the following centuries, the house was a bishop's residence, and in 1632 Sir Henry Williams, whose coat of arms with its motto 'Gloriam dei Cano' still adorns the south entrance gate, rebuilt it in classic Jacobean manor style.

One of the later owners, Mrs. Archibald Christy,

the wife of the famous London milliner, invited Clough Williams-Ellis, the architect who would later design world-famous Portmeirion on the Welsh coast as an Italian village, to redesign the manor house in Edwardian style, keeping certain features such as the southern Jacobean porch.

Built in local stone under a slate roof so heavy it had to be supported by iron beams, it was to be an example of a typically English manor house.

And this is what attracted Sir Bernard Ashley, co-founder of Laura Ashley, who had a passion for hotels.

He bought the estate in 1987 and after three years'

renovation, he opened one of the most beautiful hotels in Britain.

A portrait of an Edwardian lady welcomes you with a smile when you enter the Great Hall.

The portrait gallery and the monumental carved wood staircase lead you through a splendid corridor to the 23 rooms, each one different from the others, but in every one of which the warm, refined Laura Ashley style prevails.

In the Morning Room, ideal for relaxing with afternoon tea Laura Ashley materials are harmoniously combined with beautiful antiques and an old piano. In the pale yellow Dining Room, Ben Davies, one of the best chefs in Britain, serves an inventive light cuisine with Provençal influences, accompanied by the best French wines.

Llangoed Hall more than deserves its Michelin star.

In the Library you go back in time, for this reading and snooker room with its panoramic view of the Wye valley and the Black Mountains, dates from the

Jacobean era. Outside, from the terrace, you can see the park, where tennis and croquet can be played, and the river which offers salmon and trout fishing.

Your hosts will also be happy to give you information on clay pigeon shooting, golf, bird-watching and four-wheel-drive trips in the area.

From Llangoed Hall, all of Wales can be explored. And since this mysterious but fascinating country remains unknown to most of us, a final trip through history and the four points of the compass is in order. For centuries this country on the western tip of Europe has been exposed to the influence of many other peoples: Romans, Anglo-Saxons, Irish, Normans and Vikings. But this Celtic culture has survived them all. The best proof of all is the fact that this small country still keeps its Welsh language alive.

This is the mythical country of King Arthur and his memory is everywhere: according to legend, the Round Table stood in Caerlon, he threw his sword Excalibur into the lake in Llun Llydaw, 163

near Snowdon, and the Holy Grail is said to be buried at Llangollen.

On Merlin's Hill, Merlin the Magician is supposed to have been born. As a child, he predicted the future of Wales in Dinas Emrys, and on Bardsey Island he was imprisoned in a glass building.

Even nature here has something magical about

it, with three national parks: the lovely Brecon Beacons, Snowdonia and the Pembrokeshire coast.

Because Wales is sparsely populated, family ties and friendships are close. And there is a strong tradition which is kept alive from the tiniest village to the exclusive Llangoed Hall: the tradition of hospitality.

33

SHEEN FALLS LODGE

In 1666 Sir William Petty, then owner of Sheen Falls, described the area as "the most absolute, and the most inte-ressant place in the world for both Improvement and Pleasure and Healthfulness"

He owned not only an immense esta-te in the very south of Ireland, he was -in spite of being an Englishman- also one of the most important and most dramatic figures in Irish history. This general-cum-anatomy professor-cum-musician was placed in charge of supervising Ireland by Cromwell in 1652.

In exchange, he was given the village of Kenmare and the surrounding parishes as his property. King Charles II knigh-ted him and also gave him large pieces of land on the Beara peninsula.

On his death, Sheen Falls and the rest of his possessions went to his daughter Anne, whose husband became the first Earl of Kerry. He built a hunting and fishing lodge at Sheen Falls, on the spot where the whirling water of the river Sheen, first forming a waterfall and rapids, threw itself into the salty sea water of Kenmare bay. Remains of this lodge have been integrated into the present hotel.

The wonderful stone-vaulted bridge over the waterfall was built in 1777 and is still intact.

During the 18th and 19th century, Sheen Falls was no more than a place to store salted fish, but in the twenties the owner, then 6th Marquess of Lansdowne, started to show more interest in this wonderful spot between the waterfall and the sea. He planted subtropical flowers, shrubs and trees on the estate, which still adorn the famous 'Queen's Walk'.

A rich Scottish nobleman bought Sheen Falls Lodge in 1948 as a romantic summer residence and star-ted to expand it. But his young wife, for whom he had bought the house, was too capricious for words: a wall would be built one day, only to be pulled down the next.

Finally the current owner, a Danish

shipping magnate, saw the possibilities of Sheen Falls Lodge, with its idyllic location, its wonderful surrounding landscape and the Caha mountains on the horizon. He transformed it into one of the very best hotels in Ireland. The rooms, suites and marble bath-rooms are extremely spacious and all enjoy a delightful view. 'La Cascade', the five-star restaurant,together with the terrace, has been built right over the river.

From here, you can see as far as the centuries-old stone bridge. In the evening, the area is lit like a fairy-tale, and having a meal here is an unforgettable experience.

Over the bridge, you reach the barbecue area, a clearing in the woods near the river, where food is grilled in the open air. Behind the original yellow-orange façade of Sheen Falls Lodge, the rest of the house is just as wonderful: a number of spacious lounges, a mahogany-panelled library with hundreds of books and reference works, a billiards room, sta-bles, a health centre and an indoor swimming pool.

There are plenty of outdoor activities: tennis, golf, clay pi-geon shooting, riding and fishing on the fifteen miles of pri-vate banks of the river Sheen. Sheen Falls Lodge is, as Sir William Petty described it, ensconced in the most beautiful part of Ireland.

The 'Ring of Kerry', a 100-mile long coastal road, leads past picturesque villages, around the Iveragh peninsula with spectacular sea and mountain views.

Killarney is a fairy-tale town and the National Park offers wonderful walks. Then there is Muckross House, a unique rural manor house with beautiful gar-dens that stretch as far as the silver water of the lake.

And we will finish our tale with a rather down-to-earth, but important piece of information: the renowned Andrew Harper's Hideaway Report mentioned Sheen Falls Lodge as one of its favourite 15 destinations, and one of the top ten country house hotels in the world...

From the moment you arrive, the staff will do everything to make your stay
an unforgettable one.

169

34

ADARE MANOR

The drive through the village of Adare, the prettiest village in Ireland, is unforgettable in itself. It leads past a 13th-century church, ruins, a fairy-tale square and a main street full of colourful houses with thatched roofs, small shops, pubs and little restaurants.

Then you arrive at a monumental gate and enter the world of the 19th-century nobility.

The greens of the Adare Golf Club are framed by centuries-old, stately trees, peaceful ponds and the Maigue River which flows through the grounds. The 18-hole course was designed by and named after Robert Trent Jones, one of the most respected and best known golf course designers in the

world. He was responsible for designing 45 of the 100 top golf courses in the world!

And then, suddenly, there is the manor itself. Breath-takingly beautiful, surrounded by magnificent landscaped gardens, designed in 1850 by P.C. Hardwick.

The building itself is of a unique excentricity. Above the entrance, a tower rises into the sky, asymmetrically placed in relation to the rest of the building.

A forest of 52 chimneys, symbolising the weeks of the year, adorns the roof, and the 365 leaded windows represent the days of the year. And this is only the beginning...

The entrance hall is overwhelming: pillars as in a medieval cathedral rise up several floors high.

The Minstrel's Gallery is more than 40 metres long and almost 10 metres high and was inspired by the Hall of Mirrors at Versailles, with 17th-century Flemish choir stalls on both sides. No less than 75 fireplaces, all with intricately carved mantlepieces, radiate warmth and cosiness in the many reception areas and guest rooms.

And those rooms are just as impressive as the rest of the house. Room 203 for instance, the apartment of the former Lady of the Manor, is a wonderful example of painstaking craftsmanship and can probably be called the most beautiful bedroom in Ireland. This leads us to the history and the people behind this dream.

At the beginning of the 19th century, the second Count of Dunraven and his wife, Lady Wyndham, lived in a Georgian house built in 1720 by Valentine Quinn, grandfather of the first Count.

But Lord Dunraven was in poor health and could not take part in the outdoor life and the hunting parties, and therefore his wife decided to have a new manor house built, to give her husband something to occupy himself with.

It turned out to be a splendid idea: in those times of famine, the construction of the house provided work for many people in the area and the result was more than successful.

Unfortunately, Lord Dunraven died before the house was completed in 1862, but his oldest son, the third Count of Dunraven, continued his life's work.

The family lived at Adare Manor until 1982. And in 1988, when Thomas F. Kane from New Jersey bought the estate, it became a luxury hotel.

One year later, the River Wing was built on, as well as an indoor pool and two conference rooms.

And so, the atmosphere of elegance and exclusivity of the past lives on into the present.

Enjoy a cup of afternoon tea in the Drawing Room, sample the French cuisine during a candle-lit dinner in the restaurant with its typical Irish charm, and finish your evening in the library with a coffee or a brandy by the open fire, or listen to Irish songs in the Tack Room.

The best of Ireland lies in a magic circle around Adare Manor: the Ring of Kerry and tourist centre of Killarney, the Rock of Cashel and the little town of Kilkenny, the impressive rocky coast of County Clare, the cliffs of Moher and the mysterious landcape of Connemara.

MARKREE CASTLE

For 350 years, the Cooper family have been living in this mighty castle in county Sligo in Ireland, which is quite unique. Therefore, our story will be a wonderful journey through time, starting in the 16th century with the invasion of Ireland by Cromwell. The young officer Edward Cooper served under Cromwell when his army defeated the mighty O'Brien Clan.

O'Brien himself lost his life in this battle, and Edward married his widow Maire Rua (Red Mary).

With her and her two sons he went to live at Luimneach Castle in Limerick, which is now a ruin.

They were happy there, and later she even bore him a child.

Cromwell's army marched on, further northwards, in spite of the fact that at the time, he did not have the means to pay his officers.

Instead, he gave them large pieces of land.

Thus, he gave Markree Castle and the surrounding grounds to Edward Cooper. Until then, Markree had been a fortified outpost of the Irish McDonaugh Clan, with a fort that was built on the banks of the river Unsin.

Of Red Mary's three sons, one died, the second was left the castle in Limerick and the third one inherited Markree Castle.

Charles Cooper, the current owner and hotel manager, is a direct descendant of the third son.

Times remained turbulent and during an attempt by the English King James to regain the throne, Markree Castle was occupied by the catholic army and the Coopers had to flee. But after the battle of the Boyne in 1690, they returned for good.

The Coopers were always involved in whatever happened in the area and they integrated themselves in the local community.

Each generation left its mark on the estate, but the castle as we know it today dates from 1802. The family was always politically involved and several ancestors represented the county at Westminster.

They did not always follow party policy (maybe because they were descended from the O'Briens) and opposed the Act of Union, which was in favour of a union with Great Britain.

Those who supported union were rewarded with a title by the King, and that is the reason why Markree is one of the few large castles in Ireland whose owners have not been made noblemen.

In 1922 the grandfather of the current Charles Cooper was one of only two of the Unionist members of Westminster Parliament who were also elected to the first Irish Parliament after independence.

After the Second World War, Markree Castle fell on hard times and it stood empty for many years, until 1989, when Charles Cooper had the brilliant idea of transforming his ancestral castle into an hotel.

The entrance contains a monumental staircase which leads to a wonderful hall, from where a second staircase in carved wood leads to the guest rooms.

On the landing, a huge stained glass window depicts the family tree of the Coopers.

The restaurant is a masterpiece and the cuisine is highly praised by those in the know.

The spacious rooms, with all modern comforts, look out on the river Unsin which flows near the castle walls, on the beautiful gardens and the park with its wealth of deer, red squirrels, otters and kingfishers.

There are no less than six golf courses in the surrounding area, and the estate itself offers riding facilities.

From here, day or weeks trips on horseback through county Sligo are organised.

Markree Castle lies in the romantic landscape where the poet Yeats found his inspiration, north of awe-inspiring Connemara and south of the beautiful Donegal coast, with the impressive cliffs of Bunglass and Magho.

Closer by is the 30-mile long Lough Gill trail, full of variety and charm. It leads past holy Celtic sites, rocks, small lakes and charming villages such as Dromahair.

Then it passes Creevelea Abbey, the ruins of a Franciscan monastery, historic Parke's Castle and the prehistoric tombs of Carowmore.

It leads past the bizarre landscape and beautiful panorama of Knocknarea, the neo-classic Lissadell House and Yeats' grave at Drumcliff, and last but not least to that other place of great interest: Markree Castle itself.

The Cooper family have lived in this imposing castle for the past 350 years.

USEFUL INFORMATION

01. STON EASTON PARK

Ston Easton, nr Bath, Somerset BA3 4DF
England   Tel. 44/ 1761/ 24 16 31 Fax. 44/ 1761/ 24 13 77

- **Room amenities:** Direct dial telephone, television, en suite facilities, radio, 8x fourposter bedded rooms.
- **Facilities:** Croquet, tennis, walking, extensive kitchen garden.
- **Activities on property:** Croquet, tennis, claypigeon shooting, archery, ballooning, falconry, quadbiking.
- **Activities in the vicinity:** Horseriding, fishing.
- **Sightseeing:** Bath, Wells, Stourhead, Bristol, Mendip countryside.
- **Credit cards:** Amex, Diners, Visa, Mastercard, JCB.

- **Restaurant:** 40 seat award winning English/ French cuisine.
- **Season:** All year.
- **Affiliation:** Relais & Châteaux
- **Accolades:** 1982 Egon Ronay Hotel of the Year, 4 Red AA Stars, AA 3 Rosettes for Restaurant, 88% Egon Ronay, Good Food Guide, Amex Hotel of the Year, Courvoisier Recommended Hotel Michelin Turret.
- **Location:** 10 miles south of Bath.
- **Directions:** At junction of A37 - A39 in village of Ston Easton.

02. THE SLOANE HOTEL

29 Draycott Place, Chelsea, London SW3 2SH
England   Tel. 44/ 171/ 581 57 57 Fax. 44/ 171/ 584 13 48

- **Room amenities:** Air conditioning, VCR in every room, hairdryer, satellite TV, complimentary fruit bowl.
- **Facilities:** Roof top terrace lounge.
- **Activities on property:** Guests can purchase antiques and unique items furnishing the rooms.
- **Activities in the vicinity:** Auction houses for antiques, Harrods/ shopping, many top name designer shops nearby, superb restaurants close by, horse riding in Hyde Park.
- **Sightseeing:** Buckingham Palace, Hyde Park, Tate Gallery, Victoria & Albert Museum, Science Museum.

- **Credit cards:** Visa, Mastercard, American Express, Diners Club, JCB.
- **Restaurant:** No restaurant, 24 hour room service, roof terrace lounge.
- **Season:** Open all year.
- **Affiliation:** Independent.
- **Accolades:** Independent.
- **Location:** Draycott Place is off Sloane Square

03. ASHDOWN PARK HOTEL

Wych Cross, Forest Row, East Sussex RH18 5JR
England   Ph. 44/ 1342/ 82 49 88 Fax. 44/ 1342/ 82 62 06

- **Room amenities:** 95 bedrooms and suites, direct dial phone, satellite TV, radio.
- **Facilities:** Room service, French and German speaking staff, laundry, car park.
- **Activities on property:** Swimming pool, golf, gymnasium, health & beauty therapy, jogging, croquet, tennis, walking in 187 acres of parkland, cycling, sauna, helicopter pad.
- **Activities in the vicinity:** Horse riding, championship golf (2 miles).
- **Sightseeing:** Ashdown Forest, Pooh Bridge, Brighton, Sheffield Park Garden, Tunbridge Wells, Chartwell House, Hever Castle.

- **Restaurant:** Anderida Restaurant servicing international cuisine.
- **Season:** Open all year.
- **Affiliation:** Small Luxury Hotels of the World.
- **Accolades:** AA Four Red Star, RAC Blue Ribbon, Wine Spectator Award for Excellence.
- **Location:** Gatwick airport (15 miles), East Grinstead (5 miles), Eastbourne (30 miles), Tunbridge Wells (11 miles).
- **Directions:** Leave M23. Junction 10. Take A264 to East Grinstead then the A22 to Eastbourne. 2 miles south of Forest Row, turn right at Wych Cross to Hartfield.

04. MICHAELS NOOK

- **Room amenities:** 12 rooms and 2 suites, direct phone line, TV, radio, hairdryer.
- **Facilities Room service:** Laundry/ dry cleaning service. Car park. French/ German speaking staff.
- **Activities on property:** Interesting garden walks.
- **Activities in the vicinity:** Free golf nearby, cycling, horseriding, sailing, walking, climbing. Hot- air ballooning. Swimming at nearby sister hotel's indoor pool.
- **Sightseeing:** Wordsworth's home, Dove Cottage, Beatrix Potter's home, Hilltop Muncaster Castle, LevensHall & Gardens.

Grasmere, Ambleside Cumbria LA22 9RP
England   Ph. 44/ 15394/35 496 Fax. 44/ 15394/35645

- **Credit cards:** Amex, Diners, Visa, Mastercard.
- **Restaurant:** The AA's Best Hotel Restaurant in the North of Great-Britain, offering Modern British food with international influence.
- **Location:** Lake District, north of Grasmere Village.
- **Season:** Open all year round.
- **Affiliation:** Pride of Britain Hotels.
- **Accolades:** 3 AA Red Stars plus 4 rosettes for food, 3 Michelin Red Turrets. 80% in Egon Ronay and rising star for food. 3+ (out of five) in the Good Food Guide.
- **Directions:** Just north of Grasmere, off the A591, turn uphill at The Swan Hotel, and bear left with the lane for 400 yards.

05. AMBERLEY CASTLE

- **Room amenities:** 15 rooms, 5 suites. TV, video, radio, direct dial telephone, jacuzzi in all bedrooms.
- **Facilities:** Room service, car park, car rental, dry cleaning service, fax, chauffeur hire car, helicopter rental.
- **Activities on property:** Hot air balloon, walking, biking, croquet.
- **Activities in the vicinity:** Tennis, golf, horseback riding, village pub, antique hunting at Brighton and Petworth.
- **Sightseeing:** Arundel Castle, Parham and Petworth Houses, Bignor and Fishbourne Roman sites, Chichester cathedral, Portsmouth Harbor, London 1 hr and 10 min by train from Amberley.
- **Credit cards:** All major credit cards accepted.

Amberley, nr Arundel, West Sussex BN18 9ND
England   Tel. 44/ 1798/ 83 1992 Fax. 44/ 1798/ 83 1998

- **Restaurant:** A la carte, Table d' Hôte and 'castle cuisine' gourmet menu by Chef Mahoney.
- **Season:** All year round.
- **Affiliation:** Small Luxury Hotels of the World, Pride of Britain.
- **Accolades:** AA Red Star. RAC Blue Ribbon, Egon Ronay 81%, Johansens Country Hotel of the Year 1995/96.
- **Location:** Midway between Chichester and Brighton, near Arundel. London 35 minutes, Gatwick 30 minutes.
- **Directions:** Amberley Castle is on the B2139, off the A29 between Fontwell and Bury

06. CHEWTON GLEN

- **Room amenities:** TV, Radio, Hairdryer, Safe, Trouser Press, Telephone.
- **Facilities:** Gym, In- and Outdoor Pool, In- and Outdoor Tennis, Golf, Spa, Sauna, Solarium. Steamroom, Treatment rooms, Billiard room, Bike Hire.
- **Sightseeing:** Isle of Wight, Beaulieu, Lymington, Exbury Gardens, Salisbury, Winchester, Stonehenge, Isle of Purbeck, Bournemouth, New Forest.
- **Credit cards:** Visa, American Express, Access, Diners Club, Switch.

New Milton, Hampshire BH25 6QS
England   Tel. 44/ 1425/ 27 23 10 Fax. 44/ 1425/ 27 53 41

- **Restaurant:** Marryat Restaurant.
- **Season:** All year Through Open.
- **Accolades:** 5 Red Stars, 1 Michelin Star And Two AA Rosettes For The Marryat Restaurant, Member of Relais & Châteaux.
- **Location:** Between Christchurch and Lymington on the Edge of The New Forest.
- **Directions:** From London, M3, then M27; Bournemouth and A337 Lyndhurst and A35 and then Walkford.

07. THE LYGON ARMS

- **Room amenities:** Colour TV's with satellite channels. Direct dial telephones with voice mail. Trouser press. Safe. Hair dryers;
- **Facilities:** The Lygon Arms Country Club, swimming pool (indoor), fitness centre, saunas, solarium, steam room, spa bath, beauty therapy rooms.
- **Activities on property:** Tennis, croquet, billiards.
- **Activities in the vicinity:** Horse riding, golf, clay pigeon shooting, archery, fishing.
- **Sightseeing:** Stratford upon Avon, Warwick Castle, Cotswold villages, Oxford.

Broadway, Worcestershire WR12 7DU
England   Tel. 44/ 1386/ 85 22 55 Fax. 1386/ 85 86 11

- **Restaurant:** The Great Hall or Goblets Wine Bar.
- **Season:** All Year.
- **Affiliation:** The Leading Hotels of the World, the Savoy Group of Hotels.
- **Accolades:** 4 Red AA stars, 3 Rosettes, RAC Blue Ribbon Award.
- **Location:** In the village of Broadway, at the foot of the Cotswold Hills.
- **Directions:** Take junction 8 off the M40 from London. Broadway is on the A44 and The Lygon Arms is in the centre

08. THE HEMPEL

31-35 Craven Hill Gardens Londen W2 3EA
England   Tel. 44/ 171/ 29 89 000 Fax. 44/ 171/ 40 24 666

- **Room amenities:** En suite. Fax, modern facilities, TV, stereo, video. Fully air conditioned. 3 telephone lines.
- **Facilities:** 24 hour room service.
- **Activities on property:** Video conferencing, massage, conference rooms, private dining facilities.
- **Activities in the vicinity:** Hyde Park walking, riding.
- **Sightseeing:** Kensington Palace. Nearby to all major attractions, central location.

- **Credit Cards:** All major credit cards.
- **Restaurant:** bar I - Thai restaurant. Shadow Bar. Open all year round. Open to non- residents.
- **Season:** Open all year round.
- **Affiliation:** Blakes/ London.
- **Location:** Lancaster Gate (close to Hyde Park)

09. HOLLINGTON HOUSE

Woolton Hill, nr Newbury Berkshire RG20 9XA
England   Tel. 44/ 1635/ 255 100 Fax. 44/ 1635/ 255 075

- **Room amenities:** Direct dial telephone, trouser press, hairdryer, bath robes, fresh fruit & flowers, Crabtree & Evelyn toiletries, colour TV.
- **Facilities:** Outdoor and indoor swimming pool, snooker room, tennis, croquet, 24 acres gardens and parkland, wheelchair access, lift, helipad.
- **Activities in the vicinity:** Shooting, fishing, horseracing (Newbury racecourse 10 min), horseriding, golf (10 min).
- **Sightseeing:** Highclere Castle, Stonehenge, Salisbury and Winchester, Oxford (45 min), Bath (1hr).
- **Credit cards:** Amex, Access/ Delta, Mastercard, Visa, Diners.
- **Restaurant:** 50 cover restaurant in two dining rooms.
- **Season:** We are open all year round.
- **Affiliation:** None. Privately owned and family run.

- **Accolades:** AA 3 Red Stars, AA Rosettes for Cuisine, Egon Ronay Visa Guide 85% (in the top ten luxury Country House Hotels in England), Andrew Harper's Hideaway Report (1996 Grand Ward Winner "Hideaway of the Year" one of the only 9 hotels in Europe), Michelin 3 Red Turrets, Egon Ronay "New World Wine Cellar of the Year" award (held since 1995), The Which? Hotel Guide "Country Hotel of the Year 1995."
- **Location:** Heathrow Airport (45 min), 1 hr drive from Central London or direct line from Newbury to Paddington (45 min), 3 miles south of market town of Newbury.
- **Directions:** Follow A343 towards Andover for 3 miles, then follow signs all the way for Woolton Hill and Hollington Herb Garden.

10. THE CHESTER GROSVENOR

Chester CH1 1LT
England   Tel. 44/ 1244/ 32 40 24 Fax. 44/ 1244/ 31 32 46

- **Room amenities:** En suite bathroom and shower, telephone, TV with satellite channels, radio, trouser press, minibar, air• conditioning.
- **Facilities:** 24 hour room service, valet service, Business Centre, conference facilities for up to 200.
- **Activities:** on property Mini gymnasium, sauna, solarium.
- **Activities in the vicinity:** Golf, tennis, fishing, hill walking, sailing, shopping, theatre.
- **Sightseeing:** Roman walls and amphitheatre, Tudor Georgian and Victorian buildings, unique shopping "Rows", 12th century Cathedral, North Wales and Cheshire scenery.
- **Credit cards:** All major cards

- **Restaurant:** The Arcle (gourmet restaurant with a Michelin star), regular special gourmet events. La Brasserie (Parisian style restaurant).
- **Season:** All year, closed Christmas Day and Boxing Day.
- **Affiliation:** Small Luxury Hotels of the World.
- **Accolades:** AA 4 Red Stars and 3 Rosettes for food. RAC Blue Ribbon. 1 Michelin Star and 5 turrets. ETB 5 Gold Crowns Deluxe.
- **Location:** Centre of Chester. 35 min. drive from Manchester and 30 min. from Liverpool int.airport.
- **Directions:** From M53 follow signs for Chester and city centre. The hotel is situated on Eastgate Street, next to clock tower.

11. GIDLEIGH PARK

Chagford, Devon TQ13 8HH
England   Tel. 44/ 1647/ 43 23 67 Fax. 44/ 1647/ 43 25 74

- **Room amenities:** TV, radio, telephone, antiques, bathrobes etc.
- **Activities on property:** Croquet, tennis, putting "course"
- **Activities in the vicinity:** Walking + riding on Dartmoor, golf 5 min.
- **Sightseeing:** Castle Drog + Cothele (National Trust) Gardens
- **Credit cards:** Amex, Visa, Master, Diners

- **Season:** Year round
- **Affiliation:** Relais & Châteaux
- **Accolades:** Michelin Star, Egon Ronay Hotel of the Year. The Times Hotel Restaurant of the Year etc.
- **Directions:** From London, M4 and M5; after Exeter take A30, then A382 direction Chagford.

12. THE DEVONSHIRE ARMS & COUNTRY CLUB

- **Room amenities:** En suite, tea/ coffee, telephone, television, iron & ironing board, trouser press, hairdryer, 24hr room service, laundry.
- **Facilities:** Restaurant, pub, cocktail bar, leisure club.
- **Activities on property:** Swimming, fitness centre, beauticians, massage, steam & sauna, plunge pool, sunbed, fishing, cricket, hawking.
- **Activities in the vicinity:** Golf, ballooning, shooting.
- **Sightseeing:** Fountains Abbey, Bolton Abbey, York, Harrogate etc. Yorkshire Dales

Bolton Abbey, Skipton North Yorkshire BD23 6AJ
England   Tel. 44/ 1756/ 71 04 41 Fax. 44/ 1756/ 71 05 64

- **Credit cards:** All major credit cards.
- **Restaurant:** 2 AA Rosettes.
- **Season:** Open all year round.
- **Accolades:** 3 AA Red Stars. 2 Rosettes. 24hr room service, laundry.
- **Location:** Yorkshire Dales
- **Directions:** On the B6160 to Bolton Abbey, 250 yards north from its roundabout junction with the A59 Skipton to Harrogate Road.

13. TYLNEY HALL

- **Room amenities:** En suite bathroom, direct dial telephone, hairdryer, trousser press, radio, alarm, satellite television
- **Facilities:** 12 meeting rooms (up to 100 guests) for meeting, dining and functions. 110 bedrooms and suites
- **Activities on property:** Indoor and outdoor swimming pool, jacuzzi, 2 outdoor tennis courts, snooker room, gymnasium, sauna, beauty treaments and stress therapy. Clay pigeon shooting, archery, falconry, helicopter flights, hot air ballooning, treasure hunt
- **Activities in the vicinity:** Horse riding, fishing, golf (next door)
- **Credit cards:** Amex, Mastercard, Visa, Diners, JBC, Switch
- **Restaurant:** Oak Room restaurant open for non-residents

Rotherwick, Hook, Hampshire RG27 9AZ
England   Tel. 44/ 1256/ 76 48 81 Fax. 44/ 1256/ 76 81 41

- **Sightseeing;** Manors and castles such as Stratfield Saye House, The Vyne, Broadlands, Basing House, Highclere Castle. Beaulieu, National Motor Museum. Whitchurch Silk Mill, last working mill in the South. Mary Rose, Henry's VIII's flagship, Stonehenge. Royal Botanic Gardens Kew...
- **Season:** Open all year
- **Affiliation:** Small Luxury Hotels
- **Accolades:** AA 4x Red Stars + 2x Rosettes, RAC Blue Ribbon, AA Care + Courtesy
- **Location:** Basingstoke, Hampshire, One hour drive from Central London. 40 min. drive from Heathrow airport
- **Directions:** 5 minutes from junction 5 of the M3. 15 minutes from junction 11 of the M4. 30 minutes from the M25

14. CHARLTON HOUSE

- **Room amenities:** All en suite, all individually decorated in Mulberry furnishings & fabrics.
- **Facilities:** Telephone, 24hr room service.
- **Activities on property:** Sauna + plunge pool, tennis, croquet.
- **Activities in the vicinity:** Horseriding, Mulberry Factory Shop, Mendip Hills, Royal Bath + West showground.

Shepton Mallet, nr Bath Somerset BA4 4PR
England   Tel. 44/ 1749/ 34 2008 Fax. 44/ 1749/ 34 6362

- **Sightseeing:** Bath, Wells, Longleat safari park, Glastonbury.
- **Credit cards:** All major cards.
- **Restaurant:** Full Table d' Hôte and A la Carte menus.
- **Accolades:** 3 Rosettes for Restaurant, 3 Star
- **Location:** South of Bath.
- **Directions:** A361 Frome Road mile outside Shepton Mallet.

15. THE STAFFORD

- **Room amenities:** All rooms air-conditioned and refurbished in 1996.
- **Facilities:** 5 private dining rooms, award winning restaurant and American Bar.
- **Activities in the vicinity:** The Stafford is within walking distance to all major shopping areas and all major theatres. Situated in historic St. James's area, close to St. James's Palace, Buckingham Palace, St. James's and Green Park, Houses of Parliament. Short taxi ride to all other major attractions.
- **Credit cards:** All major credit cards are accepted
- **Season:** The Stafford enjoys a year round occupancy.

St. James's Place London SW1A 1NJ
England   Tel. 44/ 171/ 493 0111 Fax. 44/ 171/ 493 71 21

- **Restaurant:** Chris Oakes, the Executive Chef, uses only the finest English products. Apart from the classical dishes that Chef Oakes prepares, he is a very innovative Chef.
- **Affiliation:** Founder member of Small Luxury Hotels of the World, a consortium of independently owned hotels of which there are some 230 around the world.
- **Accolades:** The Stafford was voted the Third Best City Centre Hotel in the World by the well respected Hideaway Report.
- **Location:** In the heart of St. James's in St. James's Place, between Piccadilly and Green Park, and although in the centre of town, enjoys a very peaceful location

181

16. LUCKNAM PARK

- **Room amenities:** 30 rooms, 11 suites, 1 lodge house (all individually designed with views overlooking the estate.)
- **Facilities:** 24 hour room service, satellite/ cable TV in all bedrooms, carpark, heliport, laundry/ dry cleaning service.
- **Activities on property:** Leisure Spa with indoor pool, Whirlpool Spa and sauna, health & beauty salon, equestrian centre.
- **Activities in the vicinity:** Golf course, fishing, ballooning, walking, canal boats
- **Sightseeing:** Historic centre of Bath, Cotswolds to the North, close to Bristol and London only 1 hours by train, Castle Combe, Longleat House.

Lucknam Park, Colerne, Wiltshire SN14 8AZ
England   Tel. 44/ 1225/ 74 27 77 Fax. 44/ 1225/ 74 35 36

- **Credit cards:** All major credit cards accepted.
- **Restaurant:** Michelin starred restaurant.
- **Season:** Open all year round.
- **Accolades:** Blue Ribbon RAC. Egon Ronay 84%, 4 Red Stars AA Guide
- **Location:** 6 miles from city of Bath, under 2 hours drive from London and Heathrow.
- **Directions:** 15 minutes from M4, junctions 17 and 18, located between A420 and A4 near the village of Colerne.

17. MAISON TALBOOTH

- **Room amenities:** 10 luxury en suite bedrooms, spacious sitting rooms, large garden
- **Facilities:** Le Talbooth Restaurant has a wonderful garden and outside dining in summer (private dining room for 20 people.)
- **Activities on property:** Croquet.
- **Activities in the vicinity:** Golf, sailing, fishing.
- **Sightseeing:** Constable Country, Beth Chato's Garden, the Munnings Museum, Lavenham & the Wooltowns, Colchester Castle.
- **Credit cards:** Amex, Visa, Access, Diners, Switch.

Dedham, Colchester Essex CO7 6HN
England   Tel. 44/ 1206/ 32 23 67 Fax. 44/ 1206/ 32 27 52

- **Restaurant:** Le Talbooth Restaurant.
- **Season:** Open all year.
- **Affiliation:** Pride of Britain, Hotel Consortia.
- **Accolades:** An AA Red Star (3), RAC Blue Ribbon, The Booker Sword of Excellence Winner 1996.
- **Location:** 4 miles east of Colchester.
- **Directions:** About 1 mile from the A12 between Colchester and Ipswich (turn off at Dedham).

18. THORNBURY CASTLE

- **Room amenities:** Trouser press, hairdryer, some bedrooms with fourposter beds and Tudor fireplaces.
- **Facilities:** Gardens, helipad, meeting/ conferences, licensed for weddings.
- **Activities on property:** Croquet.
- **Activities in the vicinity:** Horse riding, tennis, golf, ballooning.
- **Sightseeing:** The Cotswolds, Georgian city of Bath, Wales.
- **Credit cards:** Amex, Diners, Mastercard, Visa.
- **Restaurant:** Award winning restaurant.

Thornbury, nr Bristol, South Gloucestershire BS12 1HH
England   Tel. 44/ 1454/ 28 11 82 Fax. 44/ 1454/ 41 61 88

- **Season:** Closed 2 days in January.
- **Affiliation:** Pride of Britain, Celebrated Hotels Collection, Best Loved Hotels of the World.
- **Accolades:** RAC Blue Ribbon, AA 3 Red Stars + 3 Rosettes.
- **Location:** 12 miles north of Bristol.
- **Directions:** From London west on M4, to the intersection of the M5 (exit 20). Take A38 north. After approx. 6 miles take B4061 to Thornbury. At the bottom of the High Street bear left into Castle Street. After 300 yards left (of St. Mary Church).

19. HUNSTRETE HOUSE

- **Room amenities:** TV, telephone, all en suite, mineral water.
- **Facilities:** Pool outdoor, tennis, 92 acres.
- **Activities on property:** Swimming, croquet, tennis, shooting (clay).
- **Activities in the vicinity:** Golf, fishing, walking, horse riding.
- **Sightseeing:** Bath, Wells, Bristol, Stonehenge, Cotswolds.
- **Credit cards:** All.

Chelwood, nr Bristol Avon BS18 4NS
England   Tel. 44/ 1761/ 490 490 Fax. 44/ 1761/ 490 732

- **Restaurant:** 1 Star Michelin, modern English/ French.
- **Season:** Open all year.
- **Accolades:** 3 Red Stars AA, 1 Star Michelin Food.
- **Location:** 6 miles from Bath & Bristol, set in the country near village of Hunstrete.
- **Directions:** M4 at junction 18. Take A46 to Bath. Leave Bath on A4 to Bristol; then take A39 to Wells and Weston. Hunstrete is 5 miles on right.

20. STAPLEFORD PARK

· **Room amenities:** All rooms individually designed; colour TV; stereo, trouser press; all rooms are en suite.
· **Facilities:** Full Spa and health centre; Swimming pool; 24Hr Room service; In house restaurant; massage and aromatherapy centre.
· **Activities on property:** Archery; claypigeon shooting; falconry, horseshoes; mini golf; and croquet.
· **Activities in the vicinity:** Go karting; off roading; sailing, fishing and windsurfing on Rutland Water and Golf.
· **Sightseeing:** Belvoir Castle; Burleigh House; Belton House and Stamford.

Near Melton Mowbray Leicestershire LE14 2EF
England   Tel. 44/ 1572/ 78 75 22 Fax. 44/ 1572/ 78 76 51

· **Credit Cards:** Visa, Access, American Express and Diners Club.
· **Restaurant:** In house (2 AA Rosettes).
· **Season:** All year.
· **Affiliation:** An outpost of the Carnegie Club; Small Luxury Hotels of the World.
· **Location:** Leicestershire, 100 miles north of London; 4 miles outside Melton Mowbray; convenient for Cambridge and Nottingham.
· **Directions:** From the A1 at Colsterworth roundabout, take B676 to Melton Mowbray. Through Saxby, left (signpost 'Stapleford').

21. BLAKES

· **Room amenities:** 50 rooms · individually designed, en suite. Fax available, TV, video.
· **Facilities:** 24 hour room service. Full secretarial facilities. Courier service if required. Theatre bookings & restaurant bookings. Small conferencing and private dining facilities.
· **Activities on property:** Manicure, Massage
· **Activities in the vicinity:** Full health/ gym facilities. Shops Brompton Cross. Museums Victoria Albert National History.

33 Roland Gardens Londen SW7 3PF
England   Tel. 44/ 171/ 370 6701 Fax 44/ 171/ 373 0442

· **Sightseeing:** Harrods, Kensington Palace.
· **Credit Cards:** All major credit cards.
· **Restaurant:** bar Blakes. Open all year round. Open to non residents.
· **Season:** Open all year round.
· **Affiliation:** The Hempel/ London.
· **Location:** South Kensington.

22. BAILIFFSCOURT

· **Room amenities:** Colour TV and satellite, direct dial telephone, tea/ coffee making facilities, individually decorated rooms with several antique pieces.
· **Facilities:** Outdoor swimming pool, hard court tennis courts, 22 acres of land, croquet lawn, helipad.
· **Activities on property:** Tennis, swimming, croquet, walking.
· **Activities in the vicinity:** Golf, windsurfing, horse racing, museums, gardens, stately homes.
· **Sightseeing:** Chichester Cathedral, Arundel Castle, South Downs Walk, Goodwood House & Races.

Climping, West Sussex BN17 5RW
England   Tel. 44/ 1903/ 72 35 11 Fax. 44/ 1903/ 72 31 07

· **Credit cards:** All major credit cards.
· **Restaurant:** Modern French and English cuisine.
· **Season:** Open all year.
· **Affiliation:** Privately owned and managed.
· **Accolades:** 3 AA Star, 3 AA Rosettes.
· **Location:** Between Portsmouth and Brighton on the South Coast.
· **Directions:** Off the A259 south of Arundel only a few 100 yards off the beach.

23. ARMATHWAITE HALL HOTEL

· **Room amenities:** En suite bathrooms, in-house video, satellite TV, radio, hairdryer, trouser press, direct dial phone
· **Facilities:** Leisure Club "spa", pool, sauna, solarium, gymnasium, beauty salon.
· **Activities on property:** Quad biking, clay shooting, archery, horse riding, swimming pool, croquet, pitch & putt, tennis, fishing.
· **Activities in the vicinity:** Golf (1 miles), sailing, walking, climbing, salmon fishing.
· **Sightseeing:** Hadrian's Wall, Wordsworth House.

Bassenthwaite Lake, Keswick Cumbria CA12 4RE
Engeland   Tel. 44/ 17687/ 76 551 Fax. 44/ 17687/ 76 220

· **Credit cards:** Amex, Visa, Diners, Access.
· **Restaurant:** Six course Table d' Hôte + A la Carte. English & International cuisine. Jacket and tie for gentlemen, informal restaurant in Leisure Club "Spa".
· **Season:** Open all year.
· **Affiliation:** Independant family owned.
· **Accolades:** AA 4 Star, One Rosette.
· **Location:** Countryside, lake setting.
· **Directions:** M6, junction 40. Then the A66 A591. Turn left at Castle Inn.

183

24. HARTWELL HOUSE

- **Room amenities:** Private bathroom, colour TV, radio, trouser press. Some rooms with four poster beds.
- **Facilities:** Health and leisure spa with indoor swimming pool, steam room, whirlpool spa bath, sauna, solarium, gym, beauty treatment rooms, Spa bar and buttery. Meeting and private dining rooms. Lift. Helipad.
- **Activities on property:** Tennis, croquet, fishing.
- **Activities in the vicinity:** Golf, horse riding, clay pigeon shooting, archery, falconry, squash.
- **Sightseeing:** Oxford, Blenheim Palace, Waddesdon Manor, Woburn Abbey, Stowe Landscape Gardens.
- **Credit Cards:** Mastercard, Barclaycard, Amex, Access.

Oxford Road Near Aylesbury, Buckinghamshire HP17 8NL England Ph. 44/ 1296/ 74 74 44 Fax. 44/ 1296/ 74 74 50

- **Restaurant:** The Soane Dining Room. Table d' Hôte and A la Carte menus. 3 AA rosettes.
- **Season:** Open all year.
- **Affiliation:** Relais & Châteaux
- **Accolades:** AA 4 Red Stars 3 Rosettes. RAC Blue Ribbon. 1997 Good Hotel Guide Cesar Award for 'Country House Hotel of the Year'.
- **Location:** Rural Buckinghamshire, 2 miles from Aylesbury, 50 miles from London, 21 miles from Oxford, 35 miles Heathrow. Railway Station at Aylesbury with regular service from London (1 hour).
- **Directions:** From London, the M40/ junction 7. Then the A329/ A418 direction Thame/ Aylesbury.

25. THE GREENWAY

- **Room amenities:** 19 luxury bedrooms incl. 1 four poster. All private bathrooms, direct dial phones, radio, TV + satellite, bath robes.
- **Facilities:** Room service, laundry/ dry cleaning, car park, beautiful historic gardens.
- **Activities on property:** Croquet, country walks.
- **Activities in the vicinity:** Horse riding, clay shooting, golf, swimming, biking, country walks, tennis.
- **Sightseeing:** Cotswold villages, Shakespeare country, Forest of Dean, Sudeley Castle, Gloucester Historic Docks, Bath, Oxford.
- **Credit Cards:** Amex, Visa, Diners, Mastercard, Switch.

Shurdington, Cheltenham Gloucestershire GL51 5UG England Tel. 44/ 1242/ 86 23 52 Fax. 44/ 1242/ 86 27 80

- **Restaurant:** Award winning, AA 3 rosettes, traditional English country house with European influence, outstanding wine list, private dining facilities available.
- **Season:** All year round.
- **Affiliation:** Pride of Britain.
- **Accolades:** AA 3 red stars. AA 3 rosettes. RAC Blue Ribbon.
- **Location:** 2 miles from Cheltenham town centre. Rural. 10 acres of gardens and grounds.
- **Directions:** On the outskirts of Cheltenham off the A46 Cheltenham Stroud road.

26. THE LONDON OUTPOST OF THE CARNEGIE CLUB

- **Room amenities:** Room tray with decanters of gin, whisky, and vodka; trouser press; cable television; direct dial telephone; and pure linen sheets.
- **Activities in the vicinity:** Horse riding Hyde Park; theatre and musicals at Victoria; excellent shopping all around; fantastic restaurants nearby.
- **Sightseeing:** Various museums including The Victoria and Albert Museum, The Natural History Museum; the Tate Gallery; The Queen's Gallery; and Buckingham Palace. Also, very close to the centre of London and all its attractions.

69 Cadogan Gardens London SW3 2RB England Tel. 44/ 171/ 589 73 33 Fax. 44/ 171/ 581 49 58

- **Facilities:** Laundry and dry cleaning service available.
- **Credit cards:** Mastercard, Visa, American Express and Diners Club.
- **Season:** Open all year.
- **Affiliation:** Small Luxury Hotels of the World.
- **Location:** Just off the King's Road, next to Sloane Square. Set in the residential Cadogan Gardens. Close to The West End and the City. Easier to reach from Heathrow than many more central or northern hotels.

27. ETTINGTON PARK

- **Room amenities:** All rooms are on suite, many with separate shower. Trouser press, hairdryer, complimentary tea and coffee making facilities and morning paper is provided.
- **Activities on property:** Indoor swimming pool, spa bath, sauna, solarium and gym area. Two outdoor tennis courts, fishing on the river Stour and horse riding from the adjoining stables.
- **Activities in the vicinity:** Golf, sightseeing, 5 miles from Stratford upon Avon with it's five Shakespearean properties, the largest and finest medieval castle in England at Warwick, The Cotswolds, together with several National Trust properties.
- **Credit cards:** Visa, Access, American Express, Diners. Debit Cards, Switch and Connect Cards. Do not accept JCB credit cards.

Alderminster, Stratford-upon-Avon Warwickshire CV37 8BS England Tel. 44/ 1789/ 45 01 23 Fax. 44/ 1789/ 45 04 72

- **Restaurant:** The elegant oak paneled Oak Restaurant offering modern British cuisine with extensive wine list.
- **Season:** Throughout the year, special themed Christmas and New Year programmes.
- **Accolades:** Voted one of the most Romantic Hotels by the AA. Merit awards by the RAC for Comfort, Hospitality and Service. 2 Rosettes for cuisine.
- **Location:** Railway station Stratford- upon- Avon 5 miles. Birmingham International 26 miles, Heathrow 90 miles.
- **Directions:** Located 5 miles south of Stratford- upon- Avon along the A3400, after the village of Alderminster on the left hand side.

28. THE ROMAN CAMP

- **Room amenities:** Tea making, Log effect fires some rooms. Complimentary Sherry & Mineral water, fresh cut flowers.
- **Facilities:** 14 bedrooms all with en suite facilities, TV, radio. Direct dial telephone.
- **Activities on property:** Private Fishing on 1km river flowing through the hotel garden.
- **Activities in the vicinity:** Golf, fishing, cycling, water skiing, windsurfing, sailing, hill climbing, horse riding, walking, game shooting, stalking, tennis.
- **Credit cards:** Mastercard, Visa, Amex, Diners.
- **Season Open:** All Year.
- **Restaurant:** Open for Lunch & Dinner, Modern Scottish cooking,

Callendar, Perthshire FK17 8BG
Scotland   Tel. 44/ 1877/ 33 00 03 Fax. 44/ 1877/ 33 15 33

- **Sightseeing:** Trossachs Area, Stirling Castle and 10 other castles within 30 minutes journey, Wallace Monument, Doune Motor Museum, Bannockburn battle ground, Scotch Whisky Distilleries, Museums,
- **Affiliation:** AA 3 Star and two Rosettes for food. RAC 3 Star and com mendations for food & service. Recommended by many leading guides.
- **Location:** One hour from Edinburgh & Glasgow.
- **Directions:** While heading north on the A84 from Stirling, turn left at the east end of Callander Main Street between two pink cottages. Travel down a three hundred yard drive into 20 acres of private gardens on the banks of the river Teigh and the Roman Camp Country House.

29. KINNAIRD

Kinnaird Estate by Dunkeld Perthshire PH8 0LB
Scotland   Ph. 44/ 1796/ 48 24 40 Fax. 44/ 1796/ 48 22 89

- **Room amenities:** 1 suite, 8 rooms, 8 guest cottages.
- **Facilities:** Room service, satellite TV, direct dial phones, laundry service.
- **Activities on property:** Tennis courts, billiards, hill loch fishing, salmon fishing.
- **Activities in the vicinity:** Walking, horse-riding.
- **Sightseeing:** Scone Palace, Glamis Castle, Blair Castle.
- **Credit cards:** Mastercard, Visa, Amex.

- **Season:** Open all year. Closed Mon., Tues. + Wed. during January and February.
- **Affiliation:** Relais & Châteaux.
- **Accolades:** RAC Blue Ribbon, 3 AA Red Stars.
- **Location:** 7 miles N.W. of Dunkeld.
- **Directions:** Situated on the B898.

30. BALBIRNIE HOUSE

Balbirnie Park, Markinch, by Glenrothes, Fyfe KY7 6NE
Scotland   Tel. 44/ 1592/ 61 00 66 Fax. 44/ 1592/ 61 05 29

- **Room amenities:** 30 individually designed bedrooms and suites (direct phone line, satellite TV).
- **Facilities:** 24 hour room service, laundry valet service, car park, concierge service.
- **Activities on property:** Doorstep within the park a challenging 18 hole course, snooker room, croquet, old library.
- **Activities in the vicinity:** Outstanding golf opportunities, horse riding, clay pigeon shooting, off road driving, falconry, fishing, motor racing, tennis.
- **Sightseeing:** hour driving from St. Andrews, Edinburgh, many stately homes and castles and the East Neuk.

- **Credit cards:** All major credit cards accepted.
- **Restaurant:** Outstanding traditional Scottish cooking. Recent award for 'Scottish Restaurant of the Year.'
- **Season:** Open all year round.
- **Affiliation:** Small Luxury Hotels of the World. Pride of Britain.
- **Accolades:** Taste of Scotland 1996 Hotel of the Year.
- **Location:** In the heart of Fife. Only hour from Edinburgh airport. Chauffeur transport easily arranged. Markinch train station 5 min.
- **Directions:** Take junction 3 off the M90. Follow signs for A92 (Glenrothes/ Tay road bridge). Past Glenrothes, take B9130 to right. Balbirnie is second on left.

31. ARDANAISEIG HOTEL

Kilchrenan by Talnuilt Argyll PA35 1HE
Scotland   Tel. 44/ 1866/ 83 33 33 Fax. 44/ 1866/ 83 32 22

- **Room amenities:** Direct dial telephones, TV, tea & coffee, antiques, aromatherapy oils, master loch view suites
- **Facilities:** En suite bathrooms, gardens (award winning).
- **Activities on property:** Tennis, fishing, boating, croquet, snooker, walking, (archery & clay shooting by arrangement).
- **Activities in the vicinity:** Mountain biking, shooting, fishing, climbing, archaeology.
- **Sightseeing:** Inner Hebrides, Iona & Mull, Inveraray Castle, Glencoe, Ben Nevis.
- **Credit cards:** Amex, Diners, Visa, Mastercard.

- **Restaurant:** Yes.
- **Season:** All year, except January.
- **Affiliation:** Scotland Commended Hotel, Best Loved Hotels of the World, Scottish Tourist Board 4 Crown Highly Commended.
- **Accolades:** AA RAC 3 Stars plus Merit Award, The Good Hotel Guide, AA Romantic Hotel of the Year.
- **Location:** Glasgow 90 miles (2Hrs), most scenic drive possible in Britain.
- **Directions:** A85 to Oban, then the B845 to Kilchrenan and on to Ardanaiseig.

185

32. LLANGOED HALL

- **Room amenities:** 23 individually designed bedrooms + suites, decanters of sherry in rooms, satellite TV, radio, telephone.
- **Facilities:** 2 helicopter landing pads, 17 acres of gardens and parkland, 3 drawing rooms, library and restaurant, orangery for exclusive conferences.
- **Activities on property:** Snooker room, croquet, tennis court, maze and walled garden, fishing + clay pigeon shooting.
- **Activities in the vicinity:** Golf, walking in National Park, gliding, off road 4 wheel drive.
- **Sightseeing:** Hay on Wye (largest collection of book shops in the world), Raglan Castle.
- **Credit cards:** Amex, Diners, Visa, Mastercard, JCB

Brecon Powys LD3 OYP
Wales   Tel. 44/ 1874/ 75 45 25 Fax. 44/ 1874/ 75 45 45

- **Restaurant:** 50 cover restaurant in two rooms, A la Carte +Table d' Hôte menus for lunch and dinner. Michelin Star.
- **Season:** Open all year.
- **Affiliation:** Ashley House Hotels, Small Luxury Hotels of the World.
- **Accolades:** 4 Red Stars AA, Blue Ribbon RAC, 5 Crown Deluxe Wales Tourist Board, Michelin Star + 3AA Rosettes for cuisine.
- **Location:** Located in the beautiful Wye Valley.
- **Directions:** 1 mile north of village of Llyswen on the A470.

33. SHEEN FALLS LODGE

- **Room amenities:** Remote control VCR and TV, hairdryer, shaving mirror, trouser press, safe, iron + ironing board, 3 telephones.
- **Facilities:** Library, billiard room, barbecue, helipad, health + fitness centre including swimming pool (indoor), massage, beautician, conference centre, wine cellar.
- **Activities on property:** Horseriding, fishing, cycling, croquet, clay shooting, walking, tennis.
- **Activities in the vicinity:** Deep sea fishing, boating, sailing, golf, diving, waterskiing, walking.
- **Sightseeing:** Ring of Kerry, Garnish Island, Ring of Beara, Derreen Gardens, Muckross House, Dingle Peninsula.

Kenmare, Co Kerry
Ireland   Tel. 353/ 64/ 41600 Fax. 353/ 64/ 41386

- **Credit cards:** Mastercard, Visa, American Express, Diners.
- **Restaurant:** La Cascade one Michelin Star oscars, Bistro.
- **Season:** February 1 to November 30 December 23 to January 2.
- **Affiliation:** Relais & Châteaux.
- **Accolades:** AA Hotel Inspectors "Hotel of the Year" award (1993), 87% grade in Egon Ronay Guide, RAC Blue Ribbon Award since 1992. Michelin Star for restaurant La Cascade since 1993.
- **Location:** Between Ring of Kerry and Ring of Beara.
- **Directions:** From Kenmare, take the N71, direction Glengariff, turn left after suspension bridge.

34. ADARE MANOR

- **Room amenities:** 63 rooms (direct phone line, cable TV.)
- **Facilities:** Room service, elevator, laundry & dry cleaning, car park, massage therapy.
- **Activities on property:** Horseriding, clay pigeon shooting, fishing, sauna, swimming pool, gym, biking, 18 hole championship, Robert Trent Jones Senior Golf Course, archery.
- **Activities in the vicinity:** Tenniscourts, shooting.
- **Sightseeing:** The Burren, the Ring of Kerry, Adare Village.

Adare Co., Limerick
Ireland   Tel. 353/ 61/ 39 65 66 Fax. 353/ 61/ 39 67 25

- **Credit cards:** Visa, Access, American Express, Diners.
- **Restaurant:** Renowned cuisine.
- **Season:** All year round.
- **Affiliation:** Small Luxury Hotels of the World.
- **Location:** 30 minutes from Shannon airport, 15 minutes from Limerick City.
- **Directions:** On the N21 in the village of Adare.

35. MARKREE CASTLE

- **Room amenities:** TV, hairdryer, teamaking facilities, direct dial telephone.
- **Activities on property:** Horseriding.
- **Activities in the vicinity:** Golf, fishing.
- **Sightseeing:** Yeats Country, Wisadell House, Parkes Castle, King House, Carrowmore.

Collooney, Co Sligo
Ireland   Tel. 353/ 71/ 67 800 Fax. 353/ 71/ 67 840

- **Credit cards:** Access Mastercard, Visa, American Express, Diners.
- **Restaurant:** one.
- **Season:** Closed 24, 25 and 26 December only.
- **Accolades:** AA 2 Rosettes, Irelands Top 100 Restaurants.
- **Location:** N.W. Ireland.
- **Directions:** 7 miles south of Sligo, off N4.

WHERE TO FIND THE HOTELS

SCOTLAND:
28. Roman Camp Hotel
29. Kinnaird
30. Balbirnie House
31. Ardanaiseig

WALES:
32. Llangoed Hall

IRELAND:
33. Sheen Falls Lodge
34. Adare Manor
35. Markree Castle

ENGLAND:
01. Ston Easton Park
02. The Sloane Hotel
03. Ashdown Park Hotel
04. Michaels Nook
05. Amberley Castle
06. Chewton Glen
07. The Lygon Arms
08. The Hempel
09. Hollington House
10. The Chester Grosvenor
11. Gidleigh Park
12. The Devonshire Arms
Country House Hotel
13. Tylney Hall
14. Charlton House
15. The Stafford
16. Lucknam Park
17. Maison Talbooth
18. Thornbury Castle
19. Hunstrete House
20. Stapleford Park
21. Blakes
22. Bailiffscourt
23. Armathwaite Hall
24. Hartwell House
25. The Greenway
26. The London Outpost
of the Carnegie Club
27. Ettington Park

INVERNESS

ABERDEEN

S C O T L A N D

OBAN
31

29

DUNDEE

28

03

EDINBURGH

GLASGOW

**N O R T H E R N
I R E L A N D**

NEW CASTLE
CARLISLE
23

04

SLIGO

BELFAST

35

12

LEEDS

KINGSTON-
UPON-HULL

LIVERPOOL MANCHESTER

DUBLIN

LIMERICK
34

10

I R E L A N D

NOTTINGHAM
20
LEICESTER

BIRMINGHAM **E N G L A N D**

NORTHAMPTON

KILLARNEY

27

W A L E S

07

33

CORK

32

IPSWICH

25

17

24

READING

08
02   15

CARDIFF   18

LONDON

BRISTOL 16

21   26

19   09   13

01

03

14

SOUTHAMPTON 05
22 BRIGHTON

PORTSMOUTH

EXETER
11

06
BORNEMOUTH

187

THE SERIES
'HOTEL GEMS IN THE WORLD'

The first volume of this series, 'Hotel Gems in France' was published in 1995

Further books on the most fascinating hotels in the world are to be published in due course.
They will include volumes on:

Italy
Spain and Portugal
Germany, Austria and Switzerland
The countries of the Benelux
North America
Africa
Asia
The countries of the Pacific
…

LIST OF PHOTOGRAPHERS

WITH SPECIAL THANKS TO THE COMPANIES WHICH HAVE CONTRIBUTED TO THIS PROJECT

AIR U.K.

Belgium c/o KLM Royal Dutch Airlines   Ph. (00-32) (0) 2/507.70.70
28 Avenue Marnix 1000 Brussels   Fax. (00-32) (0) 2/507.70.00

Air U.K. is the 3rd largest British schedule airline operating 4 daily flights between Brussels and Stanstead, the 3rd London airport.

BEST LOVED HOTELS
OF THE WORLD LIMITED

England Thornbury Castle   Ph. (00-44) (0) 1454/41.47.86
Thornbury Avon BS12 1HH England   Fax. (00-44) (0) 1454/41.57.96

Publisher of full colour hotel directory covering Great Britain and Ireland.

BRITISH MIDLAND

Belgium Pléiadenlaan 15   Ph. (00-32) (0) 2/772.94.00 (reservations)
1200 Brussels   Ph. (00-32) (0) 2/771.77.66 (general enquiries)
Fax. (00-32) (0) 2/771.67.63
http: // www. iflybritishmidland.
Contact: Erik Platteau Reg. Sales Mgr.   Com/

High frequency schedule from Brussels to London/Heathrow, Birmingham, East Midlands and good connections with the rest of the U.K. and the Republic of Ireland.

P&O FERRIES

Belgium Leopold II-Dam   Ph. (00-32) (0) 50/54.22.22
8380 Zeebrugge
Great Britain Channel House   Ph. (00-44) (0) 990/980.980
Channel View Road Dover CT17 9TJ
France 41, Place d'Armes   Ph. (00-33) (0) 321/46.04.40
62226 Calais Cédex

P & O European Ferries offers up to 25 crossings a day from Calais to Dover, a network of connections to Ireland, Spain, Scotland and the Scottish Isles and package- holidays in Great Britain (see the '2 in 1' brochure).

PRIDE OF BRITAIN

England PO Box 1535 Andover   Ph. (00-44) (0) 1264/73.66.04
Hampshire SP11 0PQ   Fax. (00-44) (0) 1264/73.64.73

A collection of the finest privately owned hotels in Britain.

RENT A CAR

Belgium Overhaamlaan 71   Freephone 0800/99999
3700 Tongeren   Fax. (00-32) (0) 2/640.82.45 (00-32) (0) 12/23.57.72

Short-term vehicle rental: cars, coaches, luxury cars, limousines, trucks. 25 offices in Belgium.

191

VIRGIN EXPRESS

Melsbroek Airport   Ph. (00-32) (0) 2/752.05.05 (reservations)
Building 116   http: //www.virgin-exp.com
1820 Melsbroek   contact : Rohan Alce/ Philippe Weksler

Virgin Express, the low cost carrier!!